T0246781

HAUNTED BOISE

HAUNTED BOISE

MARK IVERSON AND JEFF WADE

HAUNTED AMERICA

Published by Haunted America
A Division of The History Press
Charleston, SC
www.historypress.com

Copyright © 2023 by Mark Iverson and Jeff Wade
All rights reserved

Front cover: The home of mine owner Timothy Regan was built in 1904 and is reportedly haunted. The looming sandstone mansion is located at 110 Main Street in downtown Boise. *IdaHistory Collection.*
Back cover: First public-school building erected in Boise, 1868. *P4a, Idaho State Archives*; *insert*: Cottonwood Creek viewed from the Military Reserve Cemetery. Miguel Soto was killed in this area. *P1970-66-7, Idaho State Archives.*

First published 2023

Manufactured in the United States

ISBN 9781467154314

Library of Congress Control Number: 2023937196

Notice: The information in this book is true and complete to the best of our knowledge. It is offered without guarantee on the part of the authors or The History Press. The authors and The History Press disclaim all liability in connection with the use of this book.

All rights reserved. No part of this book may be reproduced or transmitted in any form whatsoever without prior written permission from the publisher except in the case of brief quotations embodied in critical articles and reviews.

To our wives, for their love and support. Thanks for not ghosting us.

CONTENTS

PREFACE

When Mark and I started working together on a dream we call IdaHistory, we realized we had a knack for finding the strangest, creepiest and wildest stories in our research. These stories often find us when we least expect it. We never know when a crazy story will pop out at us while we are looking into the sundry aspects of Idaho history. At times, someone who has experienced paranormal activity will stop us while we are doing one of our Macabre History walking tours to tell us of their encounter. Many of the stories we tell involve an aspect of the paranormal: ghosts, UFOs and the occasional Wild Man stalking Idaho's liminal spaces. The more we read and talked to people while leading our Macabre History of Boise Walking Tour, the more we felt the need to document the ghostly history of Idaho's capital city.

We have found that through these wild tales, we can teach people a little bit of history and entertain and inform them at the same time. People are fascinated with stories of the macabre mixed with tales having to do with the mystery of life after death. As Mark recently told a producer from Idaho Public Television, "The perpetual interest throughout human history has been, 'what's in the darkness?'" Humans are enthralled by the darkness that shadows the earth when the sun goes down and, more particular, what or who awaits them hidden in the unseen corners of the night. Of even more interest is the darkness that exists in the hearts of humankind and the psychological deviants that may or may not lurk within us all. We explored that second kind of darkness in our first book from The History Press,

Murder and Mayhem in Boise. In it you will find stories of death from Boise's beginnings, all the way to the modern era. There are stories of Wild West–style shootouts, jealous lovers, tragic accidents and the most mysterious death Boise experienced in its history.

With *Haunted Boise*, we wanted to look into what comes next. What happens to those Boiseans who have passed to the other side? Do some of them linger here in the City of Trees, in the homes, businesses and even prisons where they spent the days of their lives? The evidence presented by these stories, though largely anecdotal, seems to show that it is at least possible. Some of the tales in this collection are well known in the Boise area, while others have been forgotten over time. Still others are being presented for the very first time in print. All of them are wonderful pieces of folklore from the Boise Valley.

Mark and I are historians, of course, and while we dabble in stories of the paranormal, we don't offer any theories to advance that field of study. We can say that consensus rests on the conclusion that most hauntings occur as a result of violence or other tragedies. With these stories, we try to establish a point of origin, an explanation that might suggest the cause of a haunting. Was there a murder in a house? Which hotel room did that person stay in during their tragic death? Or, the most obvious question of all: Who died in that building? Often, we can connect these stories with actual events, but it seems we are just as often frustrated in this pursuit. That brings me to the hard part of telling ghost stories; as historians, it is difficult to verify these tales through the historical record. Sure, we can find out when a house was built or the year a business opened, but it is nearly impossible to prove that a haunting is connected to a certain individual's death. It is, however, possible to prove that a death, or multiple deaths, occurred at a location and to also describe supernatural activity that also happens at the same site.

For Mark and I, these stories are like trying to discover those things that lurk in the darkness, pulling the details into the light, even if they don't always align with the legends most often told. A good example is Mark's story on the "Chop Chop House" At first, we shied away from covering the best-known macabre story in Boise because it is such an often-discussed topic, and our goal is to find stories you don't normally hear of. Then Mark realized how much misinformation has been spread about the events that took place in the home and are often repeated in the media. Looking into the history of the house, he discovered that much more had remained unexplored from the home's past that was almost as interesting as the murder that made it famous. This portion of the home's story is not something most people have taken the time to discover and, thus, remains unknown. And that, folks, is why we do what we do.

Just like in *Murder and Mayhem in Boise*, we include a section at the end of each chapter, "Where to See It," allowing the reader to use this book as a self-guided tour. Once again, though, we implore you to respect private property and those who may still be lingering, dead or alive, at these locations.

—Jeff Wade

ACKNOWLEDGEMENTS

First and foremost, we want to thank the indefatigable staff at the Idaho State Archives for always being ready to help. We would especially like to thank Angie Davis, Cathy Charlton and Misha Brady for putting up with Mark's shenanigans during his research time.

Also, thank you to the following for sharing their stories with us: Caitlynn and Andrew Sperry, Shelby and Earl Griffin, Michaela Larios, Alexander Haro, Nathaniel Sinclair and Brent Bunger.

INTRODUCTION

G host stories are, naturally, reflections of the place and time in which they originated. They are worthy of the attention of any historian. Moreover, tales of the supernatural from a bygone age mirror characteristics of the culture that created them, the things that scared the masses and caused people to lock up their houses against the darkness. The humans who later appeared as apparitions in paranormal tales quite frequently died tragically, remaining as lost in death as they were the moment they passed away, perhaps falling prey to an outbreak of fever or dying violently at the center of a momentous battle. Haunted houses come in all shapes and sizes; they can be newer buildings or older ones, but more often than not, something of note happened within the walls of such entity-filled abodes. Often, paranormal activity lacks rational explanations or clear answers from the past. Maybe a tenant died there. Perhaps before the home even existed, someone else called that particular patch of ground home and, for whatever reason, attached themselves to the land and what is built on it. Whatever the possible origins of a haunting, it is historical in nature, and Boise, or Boise City as it was called in the early days, experienced its share of violence, pestilence, mayhem and death. It still does.

The stories in *Haunted Boise* are not only about death on the frontier; they also span the history of Boise from as early as 1863, when the establishment of Fort Boise led to the birth of the town along the river and spread north to Camp Boise, as the fort was first called. The fort sat at the junction of Goodale's Cutoff, an addition to the Oregon Trail established by frontiersman Timothy Goodale in 1862, and the road to Idaho City in

Fort Boise. *1870–1960-1-57, Idaho State Archives.*

the Boise Basin that lies over the mountains just beyond the fort. Like the soldiers and citizens who died at Fort Boise, the other protagonists in this book found themselves trapped in time as the pages of history recorded their names before passing them by. For instance, a few of the characters came from a class of women essential to the birth of any town but faced the scorn of the very society that claimed them as a necessary evil. One of Jeff's stories investigates the possible origins behind the ghost of a lady in blue said to haunt an area of Boise that is now filled by the southwest corner of Boise City Hall. If a haunting did or does occur at City Hall today, it may be the spirit of a long-dead member of the sex trade once inhabiting the back alleys of Boise City.

Women of the evening were not the only unfortunate individuals to abruptly lose their lives. A few of the subjects of the tales told in this book died by their own hands, but by mistake. Children left unsupervised also died tragically with their entire lives ahead of them, falling prey to their own curiosity and the lack of a parent's restraining hand. Other stories describe the lives of men involved in crime and the pursuit of violence, men whose deaths transpired as violently as the lives they lived. There are also tales of tragic circumstances of those suffering from depression, alcoholism or mental illness, conditions that led some past the breaking point and into taking their own lives. But not every story of the lost souls of Boise could be told in our book.

The Egyptian Theater, one of Boise's most treasured landmarks, is not included here. This majestic building, which opened in 1927 soon after the tomb of King Tut was discovered in the Valley of the Kings in Egypt, has a colorful and interesting history, including a projectionist supposedly named Joe who died of a heart attack inside the ornate auditorium. He is said to wander the theater's aisles to this day and has been spotted sitting in the upper reaches of the balcony section near the projection room. Though other projectionists worked at the Egyptian and died, none of those we found called themselves Joseph, Joey or even Joe. None of the potential candidates behind the "Joe" haunting died in the theater, either. The Old Idaho State Penitentiary, another well-known historic site, is said to be the most haunted place in Idaho, and it certainly possesses enough stories to support that claim, but the Old Pen deserves its own book of ghostly tales.

Boise can also boast a haunted strip club, Satin Dolls, as it is called today. But in 2001, the establishment was known as Night Moves. Idaho's capital city reportedly possesses several haunted homes along Harrison Boulevard, the famous tree-lined thoroughfare named after U.S. president Benjamin Harrison, who visited Boise in 1891 after signing Idaho into statehood. The Bown House on the East End of town and built in 1879, now a popular stop for school kids on field trips, is said to be haunted. Most of the city's cemeteries also claim residents of the supernatural order,

Oregon Trail marker placed by the Bureau of Land Management just east of Boise near Bonneville Point. *IdaHistory Photo Collection.*

from a phantom horse at Dry Creek Cemetery in Boise's extreme West End to the shadows and apparitions spending their afterlives at Morris Hill Cemetery just northwest of downtown on the Boise Bench. There are many more tales that we left out of our book. In the end, we chose those that interested us the most.

Haunted Boise does include a few new stories and fresh material, such as Jeff's story about reported paranormal activity at the current Idaho State Correctional Institution, a place he worked at for many years prior to the writing of this book. The book does tell one story covered by other authors, but with our own take: that of Boise's infamous "Murder House," or "Chop Chop House," as it is also known. As historians, we aimed to find fresh source material when we could; we have included this material throughout this book. From horses falling on their riders to fires that broke out unexpectedly and stray bullets hitting the wrong mark, the throughline connecting every story in this book is the occurrence of abrupt death, the almost imperceptibly quick moment in which a person leaves the mortal world and enters that great unknown. Perhaps some victims remain unaware and so continue on with their lives as if they still drew breath. It is possible that some realize they died but choose to defy the greater call to some type of hereafter. Still others—perhaps most terrifyingly of all—are the malevolent dead, angry about the circumstances under which they lived and the manner in which they died. All of the stories speak to broader issues, as all ghost stories worth reading do. But they are primarily intended to entertain as they inform. Thanks for reading *Haunted Boise*. We hope you enjoy it. We sure enjoyed researching and writing these spooky tales.

1

THE BLUE LADY
OF THE MIDWAY SALOON

In January 1916, Officer Oliver Day of the Boise Police Department received a report of a suspicious figure in front of the old Midway Saloon on the northeast corner of Seventh and Main Streets. Despite his misgivings about the veracity of the report, Officer Day did his due diligence and investigated the saloon, which had been run out of business during Idaho's temperance movement. That movement had been successful in making Idaho a dry state four years before Federal Prohibition began. The description of the suspect given to Officer Day by four members of Boise's Chinese community was an odd one. The subject was female, with long hair worn loose down her back. She wore no hat but had a white scarf around her neck that billowed in the wind. Most strikingly, she wore a long blue dress.

According to the eyewitnesses, she simply stood in front of the old saloon, occasionally walking in front of it before turning the corner down the alley. At times, she beckoned toward the saloon as if asking one of the long-gone customers to follow her. When approached, she vanished into thin air. The patrons of the Chinese cafés in the area were alerted to her presence by the howling of a two-hundred-pound Saint Bernard named Rover. Just about every night, shortly after the start of the New Year, the dog howled, and the Blue Lady appeared. When Rover began to howl, the café owners would run out and give him a bowl of food. The belief was that keeping the dog quiet would prevent the ghost from appearing.

Members of Boise's Chinese community lead a celebration in front of the Midway Saloon, the place where the Blue Lady was seen. *P1972-201-117, Rhidenbaugh Photograph Collection, Idaho State Archives.*

After learning of the apparition, Officer Day began to walk the area every night, but the woman seemed to avoid him. Day could only watch as the big Saint Bernard began to howl and then someone push a bowl of food under his nose. His ghost-hunting attempts were frustrated, but a reporter with the *Idaho Statesman* had better luck. On hearing the dog's utterance, the reporter, who had been staking out the Midway on a cold January evening, looked up. He saw the flowing hair, white scarf and blue skirt begin to materialize in front of him. Before the image became complete, the dog was fed from one of the nearby restaurants and his howling stopped. With that, the ghost faded away once again.

Several people speculated as to who this woman had been in life. Some claimed she was a young Chinese woman who had committed suicide in the county jail. Others said she was a spinster who once wandered the street near the saloon looking for a husband. A man who claimed to be a spiritualist and medium declared that he had knowledge that the Blue Lady was a woman who had taken her own life behind the saloon nine years before. Several women did in fact commit suicide there, most of them prostitutes who worked in what locals called Levy's Alley. One such ill-fated woman was Alice Durrant, who swallowed carbolic acid in February 1906 in the area where Boise City Hall now stands. The only clue as to why Alice decided to end her life was a letter written in French about her twenty-two-year-old son, whom she was looking for in San Francisco. The letter said he had gone to France with his grandmother.

Reportedly, Rover prevented the suicides of two young Chinese girls locked up in the city jail. At the moment they were determined to hang themselves side by side, Rover pushed against the door of the jail and let out the loudest howl ever heard from him, convincing the two inmates not to end their lives. Unfortunately, Rover's days in Boise were numbered by the time of the Blue Lady's appearance. His owner, Idaho Attorney General Joseph H. Peterson, ran into a problem when the City of Boise passed an ordinance requiring all dogs be muzzled. The Peterson family tried to comply, but Rover left the house, only to return a short time later with the specially made muzzle around his neck. The attorney general attempted to tie Rover up in the yard, but the dog's howls disturbed the entire neighborhood, so Rover was brought into the house, where he smashed up every dish the family owned. Peterson finally had enough and set Rover free. The dog catcher nabbed him, but Rover ate his way out of the dog pound.

Rover left the family home at 509 West Washington Street and became a "hobo," running between Fifth and Tenth Streets in Boise, always on the lookout for a handout. Attorney General Peterson began looking for a new home for Rover, finding one on a farm south of Boise. But a few days after being sent to the farmstead, Rover returned to Main Street. Peterson found another homestead in Star, but again Rover made his way back to Main Street a short time later. Finally, the Wolf family of Murphy, Idaho, took the stray, and the wily canine stayed happily put on the family farm. When Rover finally moved on from Boise, so did the Blue Lady of the Midway Saloon. With her canine harbinger gone, she never reappeared.

WHERE TO SEE IT: The Midway Saloon was located on the northeast corner of Main and Seventh Streets, the latter now called Capital Boulevard. For a long time, this was Boise's red-light district and is the current location of City Hall.

2

THE GHOST OF
POOR LITTLE CLARE CHURCH

In 1970, a young mother of three moved into a rental home at 200 East Idaho Street. At first, Joanne, as we will call her, had an uneasy feeling about the home, especially the upstairs portion. Joanne reported feeling a type of "current" when standing near the attic door. She said that one day, while she was taking a bath, the lights went out for just a moment, but when they came back on, what had been a steaming-hot bath a few seconds before had turned ice-cold. For approximately six months, she heard strange sounds, including the faint tinkling of a small bell, sometimes once, sometimes twice a day. When the ringing subsided, she began hearing voices, and this culminated in a voice saying, "help," before going silent for another six months.

The initial fear of living with a strange entity turned into curiosity, and Joanne went to the library to research the history of the home. There she found the tragic story of the Church family, the first residents of the home. The house was built by Frank Forrestor Church when he was appointed by President Grover Cleveland as the Superintendent of the Assay Office in 1895. Church had previously served as Boise County Treasurer before moving his family from Idaho City. According to Church's grandson, the family actually lived in the Boise Assay Office, which now houses the State Historic Preservation Office, while their home at 200 East Idaho Street was being built. Four children—Albert, Evangeline, Elmer and Frank Jr.—were born in Idaho City, while little Francis Clarence, called Clare by the family, was born in Boise in 1900.

Mrs. Frank Church and child, probably the senator's older brother Richard. *P1962-20-6708, Idaho State Archives.*

On July 17, 1905, Mrs. Church left home to go into town to purchase gifts and other items. The family was preparing for Clare's fifth birthday party the following day. It was to be a "brilliant children's party," but while she was out, Elmer, thirteen, and little Clare decided to make lemonade. They went down to the kitchen, where Elmer got busy gathering the ingredients. Clare retrieved a bottle from the pantry and told Elmer they should add it to the lemonade. Before Elmer could react, Clare took a big swig of the sweet-smelling liquid. The bottle contained carbolic acid, which at the time was used as an antiseptic and a cleaning agent. Elmer, realizing the mistake, ran to summon the doctor, who rushed to the Church home, only to have little Clare die in his arms less than twenty minutes after drinking the poison. The family "was prostrated" with grief, as Clare was "the pride of the household." He was buried three days later in Saint John's Cemetery, now a section of Morris Hill Cemetery.

Artist's impression of "Eddy," as described by the people living in the old Church home. Image by Scout. *IdaHistory Photo Collection.*

Joanne seemed somewhat relieved when she found the probable identity of the ghost haunting her home, but the paranormal activity continued. Visitors reported hearing a voice calling out, "Eddy." Elmer's middle name was Edmund, so it makes sense that the mysterious voice belonged to Clare, looking for his brother. Even so, the ghost began to be referred to by that name. He was a prankster. One night, Boise police were called to 200 East Idaho to investigate strange goings-on: locked doors opening themselves and objects rattling throughout the house. The boys in blue left, baffled.

After about eighteen months in the home, Joanne began to see Eddy, first as a ball of energy that spun around very quickly until the shape of a face began to show itself, the face of a very young boy. Joanne reported that her sister's boyfriend also witnessed the ball moving through the house. Later, while Joanne was standing in front of the home with her youngest children, her three-year-old pointed to the attic window and asked if Joanne could see the boy looking down at them. Another time, the same child pointed to a corner in a room and told his mother it was where Eddy died. On another occasion, Joanne looked into one of the bedrooms and saw Eddy with another apparition, one Joanne described as female and wearing a white dress. She speculated that it was Eddy's mother.

Financial troubles confronted Joanne in 1972, so she decided to sublet some rooms in the home. Two girls who rented one of the spaces reported closet doors opening and closing on their own. A twenty-one-year-old named David Mitchell asked to rent the attic room. Joanne told David about Eddy and the strange happenings, but David was undeterred. He moved his belongings into the attic but reported the same uneasy feeling Joanne

Senator Frank Church, Francis Clare's nephew. *1960, 66-49, Idaho State Archives.*

experienced on her first night in the home. The second night, a fire broke out in David's attic room, forcing him to jump out the window to avoid the flames. After being rescued from on top of the home's covered porch by the fire department, David was hospitalized with minor injuries. His dog was killed in the fire. The second floor and the attic were destroyed; the ground floor sustained major water damage. The fire department blamed the fire on old wiring, but Joanne knew that Eddy was the one who caused the blaze.

Joanne and her children found a new place to live, but not before Eddy pulled one last prank on Joanne's friend Bob, who was helping her move some salvageable items out of the basement. He fell walking down the stairs, swearing that one of the steps had been completely dislodged from its place. After recovering, Bob found the step back in the proper place. A friend of Joanne's remarked that Eddy must have hidden in the basement after the fire, as a scared little boy would.

On the Ides of March 1973, the bulldozers tore down the remains of the old Church home. It seems as though Eddy has not been seen since. The site of 200 East Idaho Street is now part of the ever-expanding St. Luke's medical campus, right where East Bannock intersects East Idaho. Even though the family home is gone, the Church name lives on in Idaho. Albert Church joined the U.S. Navy and rose through the ranks to become a Rear Admiral. His son Albert Church Jr. also joined the Navy, becoming a Vice Admiral. He headed the investigation of prisoner abuses at Guantanamo Bay. Frank Church III, grandson of F.F. Church and nephew of Francis Clare, became a four-time U.S. Senator who took on the National Security Agency and what he saw as a growing surveillance state. Idaho's Frank Church–River of No Return Wilderness Area is named for him.

WHERE TO SEE IT: The Heritage House, located at 109 West Boise Street, is of similar architecture to the Church home, and Senator Church once lived there with his wife, Bethine. Francis Clarence's grave is located in the SJ3 section at Morris Hill Cemetery.

3
GHOST IN THE CELL

The Old Idaho State Penitentiary is said to be the most haunted place in Idaho. Having housed thousands of inmates and employed hundreds of staff members in its 101 years as a working prison, it is no wonder that many have reported spotting a few ghosts wandering behind the imposing stone walls. It is now a huge museum with dozens of employees and volunteers who lead tours, maintain the grounds and make sure the lessons to be taught of Idaho's starkest institutions are not lost. These people are the ones often in the best position to experience the aftereffects of the violence and sadness from the old lockup. They often report hearing footsteps and seeing apparitions. On at least one occasion, an employee has reported going home with unexplained scratch marks on his body. One might expect all of the resident ghosts to be past inmates, but at least one spirit at the prison was just visiting the man who murdered him.

In the summer of 1951, "two ex-convicts and their woman accomplice" attempted to rob the Hollywood Market, a small grocery store in the North End neighborhood of Boise. While Ruth Sekinger kept the engine running in the car, Kenneth Hastings and William Owen walked into the store and moved toward the counter. Owen pulled out his Colt revolver and, in true Hollywood fashion, hollered, "This is a holdup!" Instead of taking cash out of the register, the owner of the store, Bert McCurry, produced a meat cleaver and menacingly walked toward Owen. The would-be robber started backing out of the store. Owen claims he did not want to hurt the man, so he fired a shot over McCurry's head. Unphased, McCurry kept charging

Crowds gather across the street as Boise Police respond to the robbery at the Hollywood Market. *Photo by Leo "Scoop" Leeburn, P2006-20-00255, Idaho State Archives.*

Owen, who fired another warning shot. As Owen bumped into the door frame, he fired a third shot, striking the fifty-four-year-old grocer in the chest as his wife looked on.

As McCurry, a father and husband, lay in a pool of blood, the trio fled the scene. Arrested a short time later in Nampa, the criminals were charged with assault and intent to commit robbery. McCurry was rushed to Saint Alphonsus Hospital but died two days later. The charges against the two men were upgraded to first-degree murder. They also faced charges from two other robberies, one at the Hideaway Club on Highway 30 east of Boise and another committed at the Caldwell Leather and Canvas Company. The gang was suspected of having committed several other recent robberies in the area.

After being tried together in a sensational trial, Owen and Hastings were sentenced to hang for their crime; Sekinger pleaded guilty and was sentenced to fourteen years in prison. The condemned men did not spend much time on death row, because in 1953, their sentences were commuted to life in prison. They were not quite satisfied with having their sentences reduced; they wanted their freedom. Just six months after the state supreme court ruled in their favor, the convicts were caught attempting to escape from Idaho State Prison. Guards discovered an eighteen-foot-long tunnel that, it was estimated, had only six feet remaining before completion. Hastings, Owen and four other inmates were placed in solitary confinement for their effort. Owen denied his and Hastings's involvement. Another inmate stated that the two had taken no part in the attempt.

In the summer of 1954, Hastings broke his leg playing softball at the prison, an injury requiring a full cast. Around the same time, he underwent dental surgery to remove all of his teeth. In September, Associate Warden Frank O'Neil drove Hastings to the VA hospital for a routine dental follow-up. While on the way back, the prison's car was stopped at the intersection of Jefferson and First Streets when Hastings attacked O'Neil, pushing him from the car before knifing the man. When the driver of a truck stopped behind the prison car tried to intervene, Hastings, still with his leg in a cast, jumped into the truck and drove off. He went up Rocky Canyon Road and disappeared into the foothills. The driver of the truck and Associate Warden O'Neil, suffering from multiple bloody stab wounds, gave chase in the prison car. O'Neil helped search all day until he almost lost consciousness from

Kenneth Hastings. #8330. *Ancestry.com. Idaho, U.S., Old Penitentiary Prison Records, 1882–1961.*

29

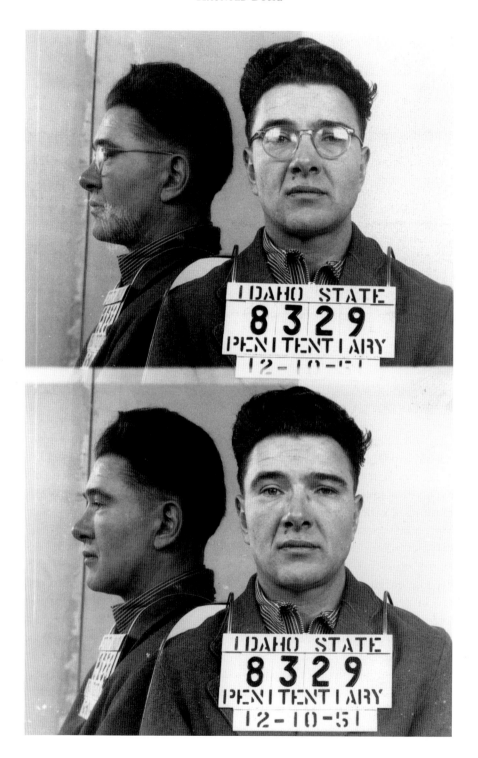

Opposite: William Owen. *#8329. Ancestry.com. Idaho, U.S., Old Penitentiary Prison Records, 1882–1961.*

Above: Idaho State Penitentiary Correctional Officers, circa 1960. Associate Warden Frank O'Neil is on the left. *P1984-15-18, Idaho State Archives.*

blood loss. The manhunt for Hastings involved sixty police officers, numerous horses, two airplanes and a one-thousand-square-mile search area.

After a harrowing three days, Hastings was recaptured approximately twenty-two miles north of Boise at the head of Daggett Creek. When Hastings was brought back to the prison, Warden L.E. Clapp interviewed him about the escape. Hastings related everything that had happened during his brief bid for freedom, but details of how and what are not as important as the reason why he escaped. Hastings told the warden that he escaped because the ghost of a man named Ivan Baker had been haunting his cell.

The ghost of Baker started visiting Hastings in his cell prior to the attempted tunnel escape the previous year. Hastings shared, "Baker sits on my bunk, grinning, but he does not talk." Despite claiming that he did not plan the escape, Hastings insisted that it was these spectral visitations that prompted his flight. The ghost of Baker, however, did not stay locked up while Hastings was absent from his cell. Hastings reported seeing Baker following him through the hills. Baker followed him the whole way, smiling always. Hastings's ghost story made the warden incredulous, even as

31

Ivan Baker, whose ghost drove Kenneth Hastings mad. *Ancestry.com user nrich0352.*

Hastings begged for the death penalty to be reinstated so he could escape Baker's grinning ghost.

The police knew of Ivan Baker, as William Owen mentioned his name when he and Hastings had first been arrested. Several items belonging to Baker had been found inside the car, including one of the guns used in the Hollywood Market robbery. According to Hastings, Baker was the fourth member of the Hastings-Owen gang and had participated in the robbery of the Hideaway Club on September 4, 1951, but had not been present for the Hollywood Market heist three days later. After robbing the Hideaway Club, the gang drove to Arco to "let it cool off." On the way to Arco, the crew stopped on the side of the road, a few miles from the nuclear reactor near the town. While Sekinger and Owen slept, Hastings and Baker got out and walked into the desert. Baker had been attempting to coerce Ruth Sekinger into prostitution, but she and Hastings had fallen in love and planned on marrying. In the silence of the desert, a heated conversation ensued, and Hastings pulled out his gun and shot Baker in the head.

Hastings provided the details as to the location of Baker's body, but the local sheriff's department failed to find it. Warden Clapp arranged for both Hastings and Owen to take lie detector tests, but the story remained the same. Since the body could not be located, Clapp received approval to administer sodium pentothal, better known as "truth serum," to Hastings. Again, despite Clapp's efforts to get Hastings to change his story, the details remained the same. Several more searches failed to yield evidence of Baker's murder, but in 1968, a skeleton was found in the area. After a close examination by the FBI, it was determined to be the remains of Ivan Baker. Hastings was paroled to the U.S. Marshals' custody in 1963, where he served the remainder of his Federal sentence at McNeil Island in Washington State. He was released from Federal prison in 1965 and died of "acute alcoholism" in Seattle a couple of months later. He was never charged for Baker's murder, likely because the testimony gained from truth serum had been declared unconstitutional by the U.S. Supreme Court in 1963. It is unknown if Ivan Baker continued to haunt Hastings into his grave.

WHERE TO SEE IT: The Old Idaho Territorial and State Penitentiary, where Hastings was held, is located at 2445 Old Penitentiary Road in Boise and is open to the public as a museum. The site of the Hollywood Market is located at 1319 North Eighth East and is currently a yoga studio.

4

A Miner, a Frat and a Ghost or Two

The Storied Past of 110 Main Street

Most of the miners who traveled to southwestern Idaho to work the creeks, ledges and mines of the Boise Basin and the Owyhee Mountains never struck it rich. For the few who did, however, some deemed Boise the perfect place to try one's hand at business ventures and to establish opulent homes, places to show off their wealth. One of these homes is the former residence of Irish miner Timothy Regan, who, after establishing his fortune in the mines surrounding Silver City, traveled to Boise to settle in the 1880s. In 1904–5, Regan put his considerable wealth into the construction of the mansion at 110 North Main Street, a twenty-room sandstone behemoth representative of Boise's own gilded age. Regan raised his sons in the mansion, but not for much more than a decade did happiness fill the foreboding structure and grace the family within. In 1918, Lieutenant John Regan died while fighting at the Battle of Fismes in the Champagne-Ardenne region of France during World War I. On October 7, 1919, still deep in grief, Timothy Regan died at the age of seventy-five before he could even bury his son, whose body did not return home until 1921. Lillie Jane Regan continued living at 110 Main Street throughout the 1920s, but by November 23, 1930, she had leased the mansion. In September 1939, Regan sold the family home to Mr. Frank Galey, an orchardist from Council, Idaho.

The Galey family moved into their new home in November 1939, and though they maintained their ranch and orchard in Council, their home base became Boise. As a wealthy new family entering Boise's high society, the

The Haunted Mansion at 110 West Main Street. *Idahistory Photo Collection.*

Galeys became popular topics of discussion for the writers and editors of the *Idaho Statesman*. Everything from dinners to card parties and charity events were noted in the *Statesman*'s pages. This coverage extended to the children of Frank and Edith Galey, especially their twin daughters, Maribel and Dorothy. When the Central School student body performed a spring music festival in April 1940, Maribel was front and center in her rustic Kentucky "mountain folk" costume in the *Statesman*'s photo of the event. Boise was in love with Maribel and Dorothy. So, when tragedy struck the Galeys in May 1942, the entire town grieved the loss experienced by the family.

On May 5, 1942, at approximately 6:00 p.m., Maribel had been playing with what the newspaper labeled a "boy chum" at 110 Main Street when the unthinkable happened after the pair found Frank's .22 rifle. Having extracted the magazine from the gun, the kids believed the firearm to be safe and so began playing with it, heedless of the danger they were in. A chambered round remained in the rifle unbeknownst to either of the children. As Maribel's friend handled the weapon, it discharged, striking Maribel in the forehead. Coroner Clyde Summers reported that the shot that killed Maribel was fired at close range. Additionally, he stated, the burns on Maribel indicated that the tragedy was accidental. No inquest would be ordered. The name of Maribel's "boy chum" remained hidden to protect the young man's privacy at what must have been a nearly unbearable moment. Several hundred people attended Maribel's funeral at the First Presbyterian Church of Boise preceding her interment at Morris Hill Cemetery. Maribel

The Galey children, Maribel and Dorothy, are the twins up front. *AP, Ancestry.com.*

was just thirteen years old at the time of her death. Though the Galey family continued to be a favorite topic in the pages of local newspapers, Maribel is mentioned just two other times in the *Statesman*, once in 1943 and again in 1950, both articles regarding legal matters.

The family continued to thrive in Boise and maintained their home at 110 Main Street until November 1969, when Edith Galey leased it to the fraternity brothers of Kappa Sigma. They moved in on November 2. The frat reportedly held dances in the spacious upstairs attic of the stately old mansion. If they were *Animal House*–style keggers remains unknown, but what has been shared by a few Kappa Sigs is that paranormal disturbances frequently occurred throughout the fraternity house. Curtains opened on their own, items were frequently misplaced, the outline of a face appeared in glimmers of sunlight on a wall and a vague spectral figure made its presence known from time to time, especially on the stairs. The ghostly encounters did not conclude when the Kappa Sigs took leave of the old house in 1975; another owner reported similar paranormal disturbances.

The owner of 110 Main Street until 2013 recalled to the *Idaho Statesman* how his children shared stories with him about frequently talking to and playing with a friendly girl who appeared out of nowhere. He would hear

KAPPA SIGMA

FRONT ROW: Dennis Gribble, Andy Thomas, John Tatro, Randy Birkinbine, Tim Englehardt, Rich McEwen, Ron Graff, Larry Ridenour, Steve Williams. *BACK ROW:* Kirt Troutner, Pat Deja, Geroge Mustard, Nick Casner.

TAU KAPPA EPSILON

FRONT ROW: Chris Bioua, Mike Canavan, Larry Jones, Don Oliver. *SECOND ROW:* Pam Jensen, Jerry Goaves, Teresa Jensen, Stan Lutes, Prudy King, Veil Bolick, Mary Lou Aourbetia; Evelyn Holt, Cheri Weber. *THIRD ROW:* Mark Skodack, Vicki Hawkins, Pat Teter, Mike Bourke, Jacki Miller, Bob Siebert, Pete Weber, Doug Jones, Glen Chase, Gary Crowell, Jan Male, Frank Vetsch. *TOP ROW:* Ed Orbea, Cathy Edwards, Tony Wilson, Steve Jenkens, Dave Kinney, Neil Gustavson, Mark Longstioth, Mike Demeyer, Debbi Demeyer.

The 1973 *Les Bois* yearbook. Brothers of Kappa Sigma are outside their frat house at 110 Main Street. *Boise State University Special Collections and Archives.*

The Main Staircase at 110 Main Street. It is on these stairs that the apparition of Maribel has reportedly been seen. *IdaHistory Photo Collection.*

the kids speaking animatedly with someone or something when they were alone, without their siblings or even a pet around. In 2021, while the author of this story led a group of people interested in the macabre around Boise, the previous owner of 110 Main stopped to join the crowd outside his old home. He shared that after a number of occasions in which his children talked to this unknown girl, he asked them individually who they had been talking to. They all replied that they had been speaking to the girl living in the attic. On yet another Macabre History of Boise Tour, while standing outside of 110 Main Street, a member of the tour commented that he had been good friends with the son of the man whose children spoke with the girl ghost. He told the crowd of the pull-down stairs that provided access to the spacious—and supremely spooky—attic. He confessed to feeling cold spots in warm rooms, hearing strange sounds when the house was vacant except for him and his friend and seeing shadows move out of the corner of his eye. Finally, a venture capital firm that called the old mansion headquarters until recently reported that on a few occasions workmen were inexplicably locked in the attic while their phones stopped working. The pull-down stairs lock in place by a hook connected to a metal ring in the floor. The tenants said that the weight of the stairs makes it impossible for the hook to disconnect from the ring on its own.

It is rumored that Maribel's ghostly visage stares at passersby from one of two attic windows. *IdaHistory Photo Collection.*

Other reported encounters include passersby seeing the face of a young lady staring out of the upper attic windows, doors opening and closing on their own with no explanation, strange noises and reports of a spectral figure moving about the place. Whether this is the ghost of young Maribel or of another unfortunate soul—perhaps Timothy Regan's son—is impossible to say. It may be that there are multiple specters. But keep an eye out the next time you walk by 110 Main Street and pay particular attention to the windows. You might be the next person to see the ghost of Maribel Galey looking back at you.

WHERE TO SEE IT: Timothy Regan's mansion is hard to miss. Simply head east down Main Street. A block down from the Assayer's Building, on your left as you head east, you'll find 110 Main Street and its many dark windows, in contrast to its white pillars near the intersection of First and Main.

5

LOST SOULS OF THE IDANHA

As a traveler's home away from home, hotels can be places of respite and refuge. But hotels often offer a sinister side, hidden behind their striking architecture and beautifully decorated interiors. Old hotels have a tendency to carry the imprints of tragedies that stain their vacant rooms and empty corridors once filled with life. The Idanha is no exception. Since this historical icon became Boise's premier hotel, opening on January 1, 1901, the stately building has witnessed its share of heartache and death. The French chateau design of the Idanha, a popular style of the period, plays a part in producing the spooky appearance the prominent structure has at night. It is not difficult to imagine peering up at one of the four conical towers and seeing the pale face of a long-dead resident looking back. In its heyday, the Idanha provided its guests with the most luxurious accommodations in Boise, before the opening of the Owyhee Hotel in 1910. The layout included a dining room, a well-supplied bar, a dumbwaiter to keep card players and politicians alike supplied with libation, a large fireplace in the lobby for winter comfort, a balcony on the second floor and a senatorial suite. In 1903, after a remodel, the Idanha boasted 200 rooms, a considerable increase from the 120 rooms the hotel possessed before. Over the years, many guests came and went, locals shopped at the pharmacy once housed within the hotel and those out on the town enjoyed drinks at the wood-paneled bar, frequently accompanied by music.

Among the notable events that took place within the walls of the hotel was a speech given by Senator William Borah from the second-floor terrace

Idanha Hotel Lobby and Bar in the 1910s. *79-22-2, Idaho State Archives.*

over Main Street on October 2, 1907, before a large crowd of enthusiastic supporters after the senator had been vindicated of allegedly defrauding the government. Three presidents enjoyed the Idanha's comforts while visiting Boise: Benjamin Harrison, shortly before his death; Theodore Roosevelt; and William Howard Taft. Boise saw the "Trial of the Century" in 1907, after assassin Harry Orchard and, allegedly, union labor leader "Big" Bill Haywood, blew up former Governor Frank Steunenberg by attaching explosives to the front gate of his house in Caldwell, Idaho. The deed came in response to Steunenberg's role in breaking up miners' strikes waged around Wallace in North Idaho in 1899. During the trial, famed lawyer Clarence Darrow stayed at the Idanha for a time, as did many of those working or reporting on the case. But darker dramas played out within the walls of the Idanha, and, it is said, these tragic events produced several resident spirits fond of making occasional bumps in the night.

One of the most horrific events to occur at the hotel concerned the melancholic last moments of Alexander Palmer Jacobs, the forty-two-year-old son of Boise pioneer and merchant Cyrus Jacobs. Alexander was a wealthy man with properties in Boise and eighty acres of ranchland near Kuna, Idaho. Family and friends shared that Alexander was prone to fits of despondency and "lunacy." On several occasions, Alexander threatened to kill his wife and then himself, once endeavoring to talk his frightened spouse into a suicide pact. In 1921, Alexander and Mrs. Jacobs traveled to Boise

Idanha Hotel, 928 Main Street, Boise, Ada County, Idaho, south exterior, circa 1970. *Id0006 HABS ID, Library of Congress.*

to see one Doctor Tallman about the "erratic mental" state they had been struggling with for a number of years. Later, Tallman informed the *Idaho Daily Statesman* that "Jacobs seemed to be quite normal" and that he just wanted "to get rid of his wife because she was spending his money." Apparently, this passed for normal in 1921. Regardless, the next night around 10:30

p.m., Alexander—minus Mrs. Jacobs—was back at the Idanha to inquire about a room. Around 1:00 a.m., Alexander's relatives in Nampa called the front desk at the hotel to warn the night clerk of Alexander's fragile state of mind. Two hours later, Alexander called Mrs. Jacobs. The nature of their conversation remained confidential. Alexander's Nampa relations once again called the front desk to ask the clerk if he would notify them should the troubled man leave the hotel.

One article in the *Daily Statesman* claims Alexander's room was on the fourth floor, while another, printed the following day, states it was on the third floor. It does not matter, because, at approximately 5:50 a.m., "the farmer of Kuna, crawled out on the ledge of a fourth story window…balanced there an instant, and hurled himself head foremost to the sidewalk below." The paper described the grisly scene, stating that "death was instantaneous… his skull was frightfully crushed, his neck shattered and his legs were broken by the force of the fall." As his room faced Boise's Main Street, a pair of waitresses on their way to work witnessed Alexander's final moments, testifying that they saw a pair of hands on the windowsill followed by the form of a man crawling out of the window, where he balanced a moment before plunging to his death, landing "in a heap in front of the jewelry store in the hotel building." A taxi driver quickly ran to report the suicide to the police before returning, entering the hotel's lobby and informing the staff of Alexander's suicide. Alexander's family believed that he had planned the trip to Boise in order to commit suicide, but they had fallen for his ruse of getting medical help, hoping his condition might improve. Alexander was laid to rest in Boise's Masonic Cemetery one year before the old burial ground was purchased by the city and renamed Pioneer Cemetery. If there are spirits haunting the Idanha's upper floors, Alexander might be among them.

Alexander Jacobs's would not be the last afflicted soul to commit suicide at the Idanha; in April 1975, John Peter Nelson, a deeply troubled forty-one-year-old resident of the Idanha, killed a fellow resident, eighty-five-year-old Joseph C. Grannon, before killing himself. Detective Ray Crowell informed the *Statesman* that the body of Grannon was lying outside of room number 410 on the fourth floor with a 12-gauge shotgun wound in his chest. Nelson, after walking some thirty feet down the hallway, stuck the shotgun under his chin and pulled the trigger; a large splatter of blood and other matter stained the wall behind Nelson's body. Nelson had been drinking in the Idanha's bar prior to the murderous encounter with Grannon. Patrons of the bar said, "Nelson had been behaving strangely while at the bar and had been talking to himself." They also said that he had been heavily intoxicated when he ran

Idanha Hotel, 928 Main Street, Boise, Ada County, Idaho, view of third-floor turreted room. *Id0006, HABS ID,1-BOISE,13-Library of Congress.*

into Grannon and an argument ensued. Nelson had recently moved to town; not much was known of the man. Joseph C. Grannon is buried in Parkview Cemetery, New Plymouth, Idaho, alongside his wife, Alta.

Other deaths and acts of violence occurred within the walls of the Idanha Hotel. One of these events transpired in 1907, when a jealous husband fired five shots from a .32-caliber pistol at one of his friends; the

Idanha Hotel, 928 Main Street, Boise, Ada County, Idaho, third-floor stairs. *Id0006 HABS ID, Library of Congress.*

man believed his chum had been carrying on an affair with his wife. Amazingly, only two shots took effect, and the stricken man lived. The victim of this crime was lucky, as one bullet passed through his cheek, shaving off a small amount of jawbone, before lodging in the muscles of his neck. The remaining slugs lodged in the wall of the third-floor room where the shooting took place. Other deaths at the Idanha noted in local and regional papers include the death of General Wilmon W. Blackmar, a recipient of the Medal of Honor and the head of the Grand Army of the Republic, due to a bout of intestinal nephritis in 1905. In November 1909, Edward L. Juneau died of tuberculosis

Wilmon Whilldin Blackmar (1841–1905). *Public domain, Massachusetts Biographical Society.*

there. One persistent story involves a husband stabbing his wife to death with scissors before burying her in the Idanha's basement, but there are no historic articles from any local or regional papers describing this barbaric—and thus noteworthy—crime being committed anywhere, let alone at the Idanha. Nevertheless, the deaths that did occur inside the Idanha supply believers in the paranormal with ample evidence for the possibility of a few genuine hauntings within the old hotel.

For those who are aware of the grisly events in the Idanha's past, the fact that most claims of paranormal activity revolve around happenings on the fourth floor near room 410 will not be surprising, nor will the contention that a particularly malevolent entity is thought to haunt the corridors on that floor. A desk clerk interviewed by the *Idaho Statesman* in October 1997 shared her eerie experiences on the fourth floor, describing how she experienced "a weird feeling….There's nothing physical unless you're really attuned to it….There are a lot of people who come in and say this place is haunted." This same clerk claims she encountered the ghost of a bellman, saying that "it was like a shadow, except it was white. I caught him out of the corner of my eye and turned to see a man walking through the lobby, about a foot off the floor." The old Idanha is now an apartment building, but the strange occurrences persist.

Some former residents and guests claimed an aggressive entity pulled people off their beds, while others reported more docile activity, such as lights turning on and off on their own as well as strange disembodied moans. A misty gray apparition is reportedly seen throughout the building, most often on the third and fourth floors. A man whose sister lived on the third floor described how the siblings "would hear scratching along the wall of her bedroom which was adjacent to the hallway, with footsteps and then louder scratching and tapping on the front door." His sister also owned a puppy, which would walk down the halls happy as could be until it reached a certain room. The pooch would slump on the ground and refuse to go on. The dog's owners were forced to pick the dog up to continue on. The most well-known apparition to haunt the hotel, the bellman, is said to play tricks on residents, hiding their belongings and taking the guests an extra floor or two up the elevator. At times, the elevator will repeatedly descend and ascend between the lobby and the fourth floor without variation. A red-haired man is also said to haunt several rooms in the hotel. Perhaps this is the troubled spirit of Alexander Jacobs or of the man from Chicago who died of tuberculosis far from his hometown city.

Whether or not ghosts haunt the old Idanha, the building is a magnificent landmark and historic treasure. So much history occurred within the walls of this incredible building that this chapter has barely scratched the surface of all that went on there. The building should be protected and treated as a boon to Boise, culturally and economically, so that future generations may benefit from its presence. What would the Idanha's resident ghosts haunt without it?

WHERE TO SEE IT: The turreted, six-story Idanha Hotel is hard to miss, with its stately spires reaching high above most of the city. The northeast corner of Tenth and Main possesses the building that was once claimed to be the fanciest hotel in the West. Times change, however, and it is Indian food or a tasty donut that visitors to the Idanha can now enjoy, not the comforts of a fine hotel.

6

THE HAUNTED PRISON YARD

It has been well established that the Old Idaho Penitentiary is very haunted, but the "Old Pen" is itself an old ghost, having been closed to incarceration for half a century. The facility that replaced it, the Idaho State Correctional Institution (ISCI), is a sprawling compound made up of eleven housing units that hold over 1,400 inmates. "The Yard," as it has come to be known, houses mostly medium-custody adult males serving out their debt to society. It has everything needed to run a small city: gym, laundry, cafeteria, church, school and hospital. The facility was designed to mirror a college campus; each building is separate but connected by cement sidewalks. The south side of the facility is where inmates go to eat their meals, receive medical attention and take classes; the north side contains the housing units. A long "breezeway" connects the north to the south. A double-razor, wire-topped fence surrounds the facility, and Correctional Officers stand watch in towers. An armed patrol constantly circles the perimeter. Between the fences are sentry dogs, animals that have been rescued from being put down and given a chance at life. ISCI is the only prison in the country to use dogs to prevent escapes.

The early history of Idaho's oldest operating prison is a tumultuous one. In the 1960s, the Idaho State Penitentiary, now known as the Old Pen, was overcrowded. Begun as Idaho's territorial prison in 1870, the structure was built nestled up against the foothills. Almost one hundred years later, urban encroachment left no room to expand, so state officials began looking for a site to build a new prison. After much searching, and even more politicking,

Inmates load their property into one of the housing units at the Yard. *P5002-2-18, Idaho State Archives.*

an area just south of the Boise airport, on Pleasant Valley Road, was selected. It was just close enough to the city to receive essential services, but a large hill buffers the site from encroaching neighborhoods. By the spring of 1966, inmates from the Old Pen were living in a temporary structure at the new prison site. Much of the labor to build ISCI was conducted by prisoners as part of a vocational program. The plans called for construction to last at least ten years, but several riots at the Old Pen forced the new prison to open early. In December 1973, the Idaho National Guard and law enforcement officers from across the region helped escort 230 inmates from the Old Pen to the new Idaho State Correctional Institution.

Unfortunately, the situation created by overcrowding, violence, short staffing and lack of inmate programming did not stay secure behind the old brick walls of the historic prison. Just seven years after opening, the Idaho State Correctional Institution experienced its first major riot. It started in Unit 9, which was then a maximum security unit, when Correctional Officers conducted a "shakedown" and removed several carts of inmate property from their cells. As inmates watched as the only things that brought them comfort behind bars were wheeled away, many of them became angry. The problems of lack of healthcare, personal safety and programming were fuel for the fire, but the shakedown was the spark. Inmates took over the entire facility, starting with the Recreation building, where the commissary was housed. They smashed windows, set fires and even drove a car from the prison industries building into the front of Unit 7. At one point, the inmates tried to access A Block, now known as Unit 13. This housing unit held mostly Correctional Industries workers, who were not participating in the riot. Unit 13 was the newest housing block, built to be "riot-proof." But the rioting inmates were able to pry the front door open and took Officer Calvin May hostage. Officer May was taken to Unit 11, where he found Officer Lynart Orr was already being held. Through negotiations, the officers were eventually freed, and the inmates surrendered without any loss of life.

The legacy of violence at the Yard was far from over. In 1988, inmates in Unit 9 became intoxicated on prison-made alcohol, known as "squakie" in Idaho. When officers attempted to confiscate the booze, inmates began rioting, setting fire to mattresses and busting holes in the cinder-block walls of the housing block, forcing the unit staff to escape through a hatch in the roof. When tactical teams arrived to quell the riot, they could hear a man screaming, but they were ordered not to act until smoke from the fires forced the inmates to surrender. After the structure was cleared of rioters, a sweep of the unit revealed the cause of the screaming. Inmate no. 14182, also known as Richard Holmes, was found stabbed to death in cell 48 on B Tier. Holmes was thought to have snitched on his co-defendants in a murder case, so the inmates on the tier broke open a hole in the cell wall and stabbed him to death. It's no wonder that a place with this kind of history has spawned paranormal activity.

Unit 9, which is currently a general population unit, is shaped like a giant, upside-down *T*. The single leg and arms of the *T* are each separate tiers, meeting in the middle in a small foyer. At night, all inmates are locked down in their cells. Corporal Earl Griffin, a Correctional Officer with five years of experience, was assigned to Unit 9 on the graveyard shift. One evening around 2019, Griffin was walking off of C Tier, the leg of the *T*. As he was securing the tier door, he saw someone walk across the foyer, from A Tier over to B Tier. Thinking it might have been his coworker, he walked toward B Tier to investigate. As he turned the corner, he found no one there and the door to B Tier secured. He looked over toward A Tier and saw the fellow officer he initially thought he spied going toward B Tier. Earl looked again and made sure the B Tier door, as well as the front door, the only entrance to the unit, were closed and locked. These are all heavy metal doors that can be heard throughout the unit if opened or closed. The strangest detail of this story is that Corporal Griffin reported that the figure he saw was wearing the same uniform as a Correctional Officer, a common element in many ghost stories from the Yard.

About a year later, Officer Andrew Sperry was posted in Unit 9, usually as the only officer working there after the COVID-19 pandemic ravaged the already tenuous staffing levels of Idaho's prisons. Many of Officer Sperry's experiences occurred in the security office in the unit. One night as he was sitting in the office, completely alone, movement caught his eye in the glass in front of him. He realized that it was a reflection of something. Behind him, a doorway connected to a small hallway with another office, usually used by the Unit Sergeant or supervisor. As Sperry watched the reflection, he saw it move. It was the dark shape of a person peeking out at him from the Sergeant's Office. On another occasion, Sperry was completing a tier check. As he walked from one tier to the other, he glanced into the office and saw another Correctional Officer standing there, watching him. Sperry investigated, looking throughout the security office, and found no one. Officer Sperry was the only person at that time with keys admitting entrance or exit to the unit, and he was supposedly working alone.

On yet another night, Officer Sperry heard a crash from the Sergeant's Office. When he looked, the office chair, which had been under the desk

Police officers from around the region are given a tour of the new prison facility, including the chow hall, known as Pendyne, short for Penitentiary Dining. Joe Munch, Correctional Captain, stands at right. *P5002-2-21, Idaho State Archives.*

when he started his shift, was now pushed back toward the wall. The chair had knocked over a wastebasket, causing a crashing sound. Another time, Corporal Griffin and another officer stopped by the unit to visit Sperry. As the three were talking in the security office, they heard another crash from the Sergeant's Office. When Sperry investigated, he found his backpack sitting completely upright on the floor in the middle of the room. He had left the bag sitting flat on the desk at the beginning of his shift. One of the scariest moments Officer Sperry experienced while working at the prison occurred in the office. On the counter in the security office was a standing desk that could be raised up and down to allow the user to sit or stand while working. One evening, Sperry watched as the standing desk, which was in the down position and resting completely flat on the counter, began shaking violently, the sides rising up and coming down. His first thought was that an earthquake had struck, but he quickly realized nothing else in the office was shaking. When the movement subsided, a new terror erupted from the Sergeant's Office. Approximately ten field mice ran out from that office and into the main security office, searching the perimeter of the room for someplace to escape. After recovering from the shock of the event, Sperry called other units to ask if they had felt an earthquake. None of his fellow officers had experienced any shaking.

Officer Sperry's strange experiences were not limited to the staff office. One evening while conducting a tier check on B Tier, the same tier where Richard Holmes was killed, he was stopped by an inmate locked in his cell for the night. The inmate asked Sperry if he had just done a tier check. When Sperry told the inmate that he had not, the prisoner seemed shaken. The man told Sperry that about ten minutes before someone had been standing in the hallway, knocking on the cell window. When the inmate looked, he saw two Correctional Officers standing in the hallway. The inmate in the neighboring cell stated that he was also sure a pair of Correctional Officers had been standing in the hallway. Officer Sperry was the only staff member in the unit at the time and, again, possessed the only keys that could let a person in or out of the block. Several other Correctional Officers working in the unit also experienced strange phenomena on B Tier. It is reported that on certain occasions, an officer can shine his flashlight into a cell, but the light does not penetrate the inky blackness. This dark phenomenon has been described as a shadowy entity that swallows the light. Corporal Jeff Wade, the author of this chapter, also had a strange encounter on B Tier. While walking up the tier one night after the unit was locked down, he saw a dark shadow walk into the janitor's closet, but when he looked, no one was there.

Shelby Epps is also a Correctional Corporal with about five years of experience at the Idaho State Correctional Institution, and she has experienced her fair share of encounters with paranormal prisoners. One night while working in Unit 10, a general population unit, she was in the staff office between tier checks. Corporal Epps, the only staff member in the unit at the time, started hearing footsteps in the attic space above her. The attic in this unit has an expanded metal walkway that stretches across the entire space. In an emergency, Correctional Officers can climb a ladder, walk across that walkway and use an escape hatch to get out of the unit. The only way into and out of that attic space is via the ladder or the escape hatch that opens onto the unit's roof. The hatch can be opened only from inside the attic. As Epps stopped to listen to the footsteps, she realized that they were coming from the direction of the escape hatch and moving toward the ladder down into the office. In terror, Epps realized that the sounds of footsteps had turned into the sound of someone climbing down the ladder. Suddenly, the door to the unit's Sergeant's Office slammed shut, leaving Epps spooked.

Another night in Unit 10, an inmate got Epps's attention. He told her he had been asleep on his bunk in his single cell when the sound of his cell door unlocking awakened him. In this unit, the cells have no toilets or sinks, so in

Inmates unloading their property under the direction of Correctional Officers at the new Idaho State Correctional Institution. Director of the Department of Correction Raymond May looks on. *P-5002-2-40, Idaho State Archives.*

order to afford the use of the restroom facilities, the residents have keys to their own cells. Only the inmate who lives in that cell and staff members have keys to that particular cell. Despite this, the inmate reported to Corporal Epps that the door unlocked and then another inmate walked into the cell. The prisoner told Shelby that earlier in the evening he had some words with a group of other inmates who were being too noisy on the tier, so he thought that one of them was coming to beat him up. As he prepared himself for the coming fight, the intruding inmate simply disappeared. The inmate asked Epps to keep an extra eye out on his tier.

Unit 14 seems to be one of the most active in terms of otherworldly activity. One of the largest units at the Yard, this building houses over two hundred inmates. Nicknamed "Ol' Ironsides" by some staff members for its resemblance to a large, square battleship, Unit 14 was built in the 1990s to provide additional beds to ISCI. There are three tiers of open, dorm-style bunks and one that has cells. In front of the unit is a courtyard, which has a gate that opens to the rest of the facility, and a large rolling door that opens into the unit itself. Both the gate and the door are controlled by a Correctional Officer who sits in a Unit Control Center, a full story above the rest of the facility. One night, Officer Caitlynn Nath was working in this control center when she heard over the radio a request for the front gate to be opened. She looked out and saw a correctional officer standing at the gate, so she hit the button to open it. As she watched the officer cross the courtyard, she rolled open the front door of the unit. Shelby Epps was sitting in the staff office on the ground floor of the unit when she heard the door open. She looked to see who was walking in, but no one presented themselves. She used her radio to ask Officer Nath why she had opened the front door. Nath told Epps that she had let an officer into the unit. Epps searched the hallway and found no one, but she would have a similar experience in the future. This time, though, she saw the phantom correctional officer walk into the unit and past the door of the office where she was sitting. It was winter, and this officer wore the typical state-issued weather gear: a jacket, beanie and gloves. Again, she searched the hallway to no avail.

Shelby's experiences in Unit 14 are exceptionally creepy. One night while working in the downstairs office on some paperwork, she got up to use the restroom. She closed and locked the office door behind her. When she returned to the office, she found that the stack of papers she had been working on had arranged itself in a perfect stack, but not flat on the desk. The stack was sitting straight up, on its long edge. A slight bend in the stack was the only thing keeping it upright. Shelby was the only person who

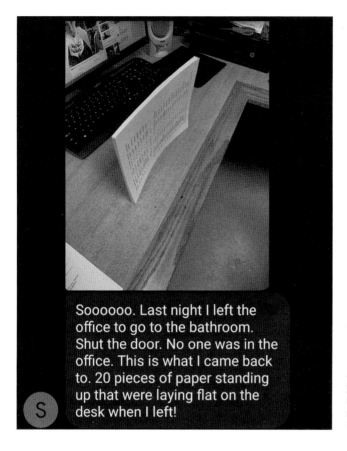

Soooooo. Last night I left the office to go to the bathroom. Shut the door. No one was in the office. This is what I came back to. 20 pieces of paper standing up that were laying flat on the desk when I left!

Actual photo of papers stacked in a seemingly impossible manner. *Shelby (Epps) Griffin.*

had the key to this office; anyone else in the unit sat behind several locked doors that could be opened only by the officer in the control center. Other experiences in this staff office include the refrigerator opening and closing on its own, water bottles flying off a table and landing in the middle of the room and unexplainable sounds.

The control center can also claim its share of strange encounters with the darkness housed within Unit 14. To get to the control center, officers must pass through two doors that are interlocked, meaning one door has to be closed before the other will open. Both doors can be opened only by the unit control officer. On a few occasions, Officer Epps was working in the control center when she heard scratching sounds coming from between the doors. This noise had an animalistic characteristic to it, as if a large dog had gotten trapped between the doors and was asking to be let out. On other occasions, the intercom button between the two doors would activate when no one was between the doors. One night at the beginning of their shifts,

Correctional Officer Alexander Haro directs inmate traffic from his tower post. *Idaho Department of Correction.*

Epps was standing in the control bubble, looking out at the rest of the Yard. Officer Griffin would often shine his flashlight at Epps as a greeting on his way into Unit 9. On this occasion, Griffin could see Epps in the window, but someone else was standing next to her. When he got to Unit 9, Griffin called Epps on the phone and asked who was in there with her, but Epps said there was no one with her. This happened again to Officers Michaela Larios and Alexander Haro during a daytime shift. Haro was working in a guard tower that stands in the middle of the facility, while Larios was in the Unit 14 Control Center. Haro and Larios were casually chitchatting on the phone when Haro happened to look over at the front of Unit 14. He could see someone looking out the window right back at him. Officer Haro asked Officer Larios who was in the control center with her, but she said that she was all alone.

Epps and Griffin experienced another disturbing incident together. While Griffin worked in the security office of Unit 9 and Epps in the Unit 14

Control Center with Officer Nath, Epps and Griffin were talking on the phone when Griffin heard a strange voice say, "Come here," during a brief pause in the conversation. It was a deep and gravely male voice. While Griffin tried to make sense of the strange occurrence, the voice again came over the phone, saying, "now." None of the officers on the phone call could tell where the voice came from. And "bleed" from other communication devices was not a common occurrence.

Unit 13, the block where Officer May was taken hostage during the 1990 riot, seems to have almost constant paranormal activity. Corporal Griffin reported that one night he was at the front door of the unit, waiting to be let in. Through the window on the door he could see a person standing near some laundry carts, an individual who should not have been there, as the unit was locked down for the night and only one officer was on duty in the unit. The figure seemed to be watching Griffin. When the door opened, the person ducked back around a corner. Griffin searched the area, but no one was there; all of the adjoining doors were closed and locked. Officer Nathaniel Sinclair was in the unit's control center at the time. He did not witness the figure but did hear a breath down the back of his neck at the same time that Griffin first spotted the out-of-place person.

Inside the control center of the unit, a spiral staircase leads down to the basement. This area contains HVAC equipment and is used for supply storage, but something else is said to lurk in the confusing maze of rooms. Officer Aiden Allen was working in the control center one day while the unit's inmate janitor stood in the doorway talking to him. Suddenly, the janitor stopped and looked down the staircase, asking Officer Allen if anyone had gone down to the basement. When Allen told him there was no one downstairs, the inmate told Allen he had seen an officer walk by. Many officers working in that unit have reported hearing footsteps coming up the stairs, loud breathing and even voices coming from that basement. This activity happened occasionally over the years but increased in volume and intensity after one of those officers gave the basement entity the nickname "Solomon" (with no explanation as to where that name came from). Once named, Solomon seemed to gain more power to exert its will. The phantom footsteps became more frequent, objects started to move around the control center by themselves and people's feelings of being watched while alone increased.

Solomon's will to make himself known became apparent one night when Officer Allen and Corporal Wade were talking in the control center. The control center holds two panels, each with four switches, one for each tier door in the unit. Corporal Wade sat with his back to one of the panels when suddenly the switches began flipping on their own. Both Allen and Wade could hear not only the switches moving but also the locks they correspond to opening, allowing the tier doors to open. This went on for approximately twenty seconds, with each lock being "popped" three or four times. Corporal Wade had been working in that unit for more than two years at the time, and that night constituted the only time the switches activated seemingly of their own accord. Fortunately, no security issues occurred.

The ghostly activity at the Idaho State Correctional Institution is enough to spook the toughest Correctional Officer. They confidently walk among the worst of society: rapists, thieves and murderers. They are subjected to low pay, insane amounts of overtime and a lack of respect from the public they protect. They can expect to be cursed at, battered, ignored by the state legislature and left with post-traumatic stress disorder. Yet most remain unaware of the possibility that when walking into the prison they might encounter not only the evil that dwells within the living but also the darkness they leave behind. Are these spirits there to punish their captors? Or are they there to serve out their earthly punishments in the afterlife? When asked these questions, Corporal Epps summed it up best: "They just want us to know they are still there."

WHERE TO SEE IT: To encounter these ghosts, you will have to either commit a felony or apply for a job.

7
THOSE HAUNTED HILLS

R   ising above the City of Boise like a gradual set of steps and leading
     to the mountains beyond is the Boise Front. These foothills act as a
     reminder of the natural world just outside the city limits. Snaking
throughout these hills are miles of trails used by hikers, runners and
mountain bikers. Visitors to this recreation area are treated to wonderful
views of the city below and the mountains above. They may also encounter
wildlife such as deer, many varieties of birds, mountain lions and, perhaps,
the spirits of those long dead. Hauntings have been reported throughout the
foothills, especially in the two cemeteries located in their shadows. Fort Boise
Military Reserve Cemetery is reportedly a hotbed of paranormal activity,
with many visitors claiming they hear barely audible voices in the little-
visited graveyard. A white specter reportedly runs up the hill near the resting
place of many Fort Boise soldiers, toward the flagpole at the uppermost edge
of the cemetery. On the other end of Boise, Dry Creek Cemetery is also
said to be haunted, the most popular paranormal claim being the sound of
phantom horse hooves emanating near the Famer's Union Canal that is the
southern border of the cemetery.

Longtime columnist for the *Idaho Statesman* Dick d'Easum often wrote
about the state's ghosts in his history of Idaho column. One such story is that
of Miguel Soto, a mule packer hailing from Mexico. In 1864, he enlisted
in the First California Native Cavalry, a volunteer group training to ready
themselves in case the rebellion reached the West Coast during the Civil
War. By 1868, he was in Idaho City working as an express carrier. When

gold was struck at Loon Creek in the summer of 1869 in what is today the Salmon-Challis National Forest north of Stanley, Idaho, a small gold rush began, bringing men from other diminishing mining claims. The 1870 U.S. Census counted Soto at the Loon Creek Mining District in August. He was probably there for only a short time to sell the goods he was able to pack into the remote region on his mules. He returned to Boise carrying a small fortune in gold dust. The *Idaho Tri-Weekly Statesman* reported that he carried around $3,000 on his person, which he planned to use on returning to California.

On Wednesday, September 21, 1870, Soto met with a friend named Carmer Moralles in Boise City. Moralles gave Soto some of his own money for safekeeping while Soto camped outside the city, about a mile and a half from the Fort Boise Barracks on Cottonwood Creek. When Soto failed to return to the city at the agreed-upon time and day, Moralles went into the foothills looking for him. When he found the packer's camp, Moralles was met with a terrifying sight: Soto was dead on the ground, his body lying in a pool of blood and wrapped in a blanket. Moralles returned to the city for help, and a coroner's jury hiked up to the camp to investigate. When members of the committee pulled back the blanket, Soto's brains began oozing from his crushed skull. A bullet wound penetrated his cheek, and his hands were clenched, drawn up as if he died trying to defend himself against the brutal attack.

Searching the camp, the investigators found two wallets, a money belt and a pocketbook, all empty. The robber had even searched the dead man's pants pockets and cut open his aparejos, the pack saddles used by mule packers to move goods. It was understood as common practice for packers to hide gold dust and valuables in their aparejos, the logic being that robbers would have to take time to unpack them to get the loot. Soto's dog still sat beside his deceased master in camp, which led investigators to speculate that Soto had been murdered by someone who knew him and the animal. The victim's empty revolver rested nearby, the powder burns on his face indicating he had been shot at close range with his own weapon.

The identity of Soto's murderer was never discovered, but d'Easum adds another interesting detail to the story. One of Soto's aparejos was supposedly found near the campfire, full of gold and half-buried. This small detail made locals wonder if more of Soto's treasure still waited to be found in the foothills. This rumor caused a scramble to find the murdered packer's gold. Legend has it that soldiers from the Fort Boise Barracks went into the hills looking for the gold one day when they heard the voice of a man in

Cottonwood Creek viewed from the Military Reserve Cemetery. Miguel Soto was killed in this area. *P1970-66-7, Idaho State Archives.*

one of the gulches above the town. The voice sounded as if he were talking to a pack string, but when the soldiers looked around, no packer could be seen, nor his pack mules. Needless to say, the soldiers returned to their post empty-handed and a little frightened. Perhaps the gold is still buried in an old aparejo hidden under the sagebrush growing within the Cottonwood Creek gulch—still being protected by the ghost of Miguel Soto.

Dick d'Easum briefly mentioned another haunting in the foothills above Boise in the *Statesman.* An apparition of a stage robber appeared at Clawson's Toll Gate, about eight miles outside of town on the old stage road leading from Boise to Idaho City. Unfortunately, in his piece, d'Easum provides no detail regarding this ghost story other than to say it had been talked about but rarely appeared in print. It certainly makes sense that a stage robber would linger in the foothills, as a few stage robberies took place around Boise City in the town's Wild West days. But there were no robberies in the area of Clawson's Toll Gate involving the death of an outlaw. One incident of violence did, however, occur at the toll gate that might provide an origin for a specter resembling a long-dead stage robber, an outlaw with his pistol leveled and ready to shoot.

Hugh Clawson, along with his business partner, was granted a license by Ada County to build a toll gate on the stage road between Boise City and Idaho City. In exchange for the permission to charge every traveler, including the sheriff on county business, a toll to use the road, Clawson maintained the thoroughfare for Ada County from the toll gate all the way to the Boise County line. After Clawson bought out his partner's share in the enterprise, the location became known as Clawson's Toll Gate. Clawson built a home for his family there, and other business activities such as logging and mining occurred in the area. Later, it became a popular sledding hill in the winter and a camping area in the summer.

Sometime toward the end of 1875, Clawson hired a widow named Serena Ray as a housekeeper to take care of his home at the toll gate. Whether she left her employment under good terms is not recorded, but on Christmas Eve, Serena and her husband of two months, Joseph Thompson, stopped by so Serena could collect her pay from Clawson. Thompson was working at a lumber mill between the toll gate and Idaho City and had previously worked as a teamster at the Owyhee mines. When Clawson told Serena he did not have the money to pay her at the moment but would have it on New Year's

Clawson's Toll Gate on the road to Idaho City. *P2018-13 GP, Idaho State Archives.*

Day, Thompson interjected, and the two men started to argue. Thompson drew his pistol, and Clawson drew his and fired two rounds, one striking Thompson in his right leg and the other in his left side. Thompson did not have a chance to return fire. He collapsed, and his pulse began to plummet. He lingered until around 10:00 a.m. the next day before expiring. Thompson had been shot before. While working in the Owhyee mines two years before, he received a wound to the neck at Colonel William Dewey's saloon in Silver City, but recovered. As was the case for many men of that time, a man who lived by the gun eventually died by the gun. For the shooting, Clawson was arrested and put on trial in Idaho City. He was acquitted on the grounds of self-defense. A visitor to the area unaware of this story might mistake the ghost of Joe Thompson for that of a stage robber preparing to fire a shot at them, as he will do for eternity.

WHERE TO SEE IT: Dry Creek Cemetery is located off Highway 55 on Hill Road. The Fort Boise Military Cemetery is on Mountain Cove Road, about a mile behind Fort Boise. Miguel Soto was found dead approximately a mile and a half up Shaw Mountain / Rocky Canyon Road. Keep following that road for Clawson's Toll Gate just below Aldape Summit. This is the route of the Race to Robie Creek.

8

THE EIGHTH STREET ENTITY

The house once sat at 1313 Eighth Street, between Washington and State Streets, which today is on the grounds of the old Carnegie library, built in 1905. In 1892, Jesse Black, the proprietor of Boise's Free Coinage Cigar Store, and his family occupied the home. Mr. Black must have been a kind and supportive man, because he allowed an employee, Daniel O'brien, to keep a room within his residence. O'brien reportedly drank heavily, often displaying erratic behavior around town. So, in November 1892, when he began sharing frightening stories of strange occurrences in his room, few believed him. But the sleep-plagued man remained adamant that some uncanny and evil entity haunted his chambers and, possibly, the house at large. O'brien described how, on the Saturday last, around 10:00 p.m., he had been suddenly awoken by the feeling of another presence watching him from some dark corner of his room. After calling to whatever may have been in his room to show itself, without reply, O'brien returned to a fitful sleep, only to be awoken once again by the violent rattling of the bedroom door and a chair sliding slowly across the floor. Shaking in bed and out of his mind with fright, O'brien seemed frozen in place, unable to move as he desperately willed his muscles to respond. At this point, he heard a faint whisper telling him the room was occupied by the dead and that they wished to speak with him. Yet once again, he talked himself out of what he had just witnessed with his own eyes. Lying back down, the now heavily perspiring man tried, unsuccessfully, to return to his weary dreams. As he struggled to sleep and remain sane, the door and furniture in his room continued to rattle.

Boise view, northwest from the Capitol toward the grounds of the Carnegie library and the haunted home of Jesse Black at bottom center of the photo. *P1962-20-3, R. Harold Sigler Photograph Collection. Idaho State Archives.*

The house possessed its own history before the Black family moved in and Mr. O'brien lived within its walls. Several people, the *Daily Statesman* reported in 1892, had died in the home before Jesse Black purchased the property. Additionally, prior to occupying 1313 Eighth Street, the house had sat in South Boise before being moved across the river sometime around 1880. In 1890, a Mr. W.F. Denman lived in the haunted home after moving to Boise City from Pueblo, Colorado. In his early thirties, Denman worked for the Colorado Investment Company and busied himself in buying up properties throughout town, including three lots at the corner of Eighth and Bannock, where he intended to build a wholesale furniture manufacturing business. Tragically, Denman never realized his ambitious plans. In August 1891, while riding near the intersection of Eighth and Idaho Streets, his horse ran into the back of a wagon jutting out from a garage and was spooked. The animal bolted hard into a telephone pole. The impact of the horse falling on Denman's right leg broke the stricken man's femur and kneecap. Dr. Perrault was called to the scene of the accident and believed the injury, while severe, would not prove fatal. Tragically, the doctor's diagnosis turned out to be wrong, and the would-be furniture manufacturer died in the house on Eighth Street at the age of thirty-four, leaving a wife but no children behind.

Unaware of the house's dark past, O'brien woke the next morning eagerly awaiting the morning light streaming through his bedroom window. After getting dressed, an exhausted O'brien approached his boss and landlord, Mr. Black, to share the unexplainable events of the previous night and early morning. His benefactor treated the story with "a guffaw of derision," the *Daily Statesman* reported. Nonetheless, O'brien persisted in his admissions and eventually gained the interest of a few curious friends and associates of Jesse Black. Eventually, a well-known man-about-town named Albert E. Werner proposed to stay the night with O'brien in the haunted room to ascertain the authenticity of the claims. On the night of the sleepover, O'brien was stricken with fear; he began mumbling and became quickly covered in a cold sweat. The door could be heard rattling loudly on its hinges, but Werner's attention focused on a "bright zig-zag of light on the wall." Later, Werner described how the light "resembled some one [*sic*] writing on the wall with a trail of fire." Werner called out to Mr. Black, urging him to enter the room posthaste, which he did. When Black entered the room, O'brien told both men that the whispering spirit had informed him that his dead sister would contact him by writing a message on the wall of his bedroom. Terrified by beholding the sight of a fiery trail of light tracing the indecipherable message on his wall, Jesse Black urged the men to leave the haunted room immediately. The other two men proved only too eager, immediately removing themselves to another part of the house to await the dawn. Especially afflicted that night was O'brien, complaining to his fellow witnesses that he kept seeing faces of specters staring at him from the walls and corners of the room.

The following night, Black gathered thirty friends, including several of Boise's most prominent businessmen, purported the *Daily Statesman*, and invited them into his home to witness the terrors of the previous two nights. The large group of people did not dissuade the resident spirits from making their presence known; right away, a loud tapping began to emanate from within the haunted room. O'brien, along with several others, entered the room, where the thuds and thumps immediately became increasingly loud. Suddenly, O'brien shouted in horror and pointed at what he said were menacing faces that no one else could see. He left the room but was persuaded to return once again. On entering for the last time, O'brien began to shake and tremble as the loud noises grew increasingly loud. Shouting in horror, he

First public-school building erected in Boise, 1868. The house behind and to the left of the school shack is the home of Jesse Black. *P4a, Idaho State Archives.*

bound from the room to shelter behind the large group of people assembled outside the door. Witnesses claimed to have heard unexplained noises coming from within the room and attested to O'brien's terrified demeanor, saying he was "suffering untold agonies from what he sees." The fact that Jesse Black and Albert E. Werner attested to the veracity of O'brien's claims provided the paranormally afflicted man a measure of credibility. In addition, a lawman of some renown, Ras Beemer, who was also at the house that third night, shared that something similar had happened at the house some twelve years before, when it was the home of a Mr. Stapelton and family at its former location. Yet another unidentified and "prominent man in this city," as the *Daily Statesman* described him, had recently moved from the home and shared tales of doors opening without visible assistance, strange noises and the presence of an oppressive force pervading the home. For those wishing to witness more unexplainable phenomena, O'brien informed them that the spirits declared that the otherworldly activity would last but three nights and no more.

Despite the spirits making their intentions known to never return, Mr. and Mrs. Black remained extremely worried by the strange affair; they moved soon after. Dan O'brien, as the subject of the entities' attention, moved out straightaway. For the rest of the decade, the rooms of the home were rented out to state representatives wishing to live near the old territorial—now state—house where the Idaho State Capitol now stands. The address of the home was changed to 802 Eighth Street around 1899. The property where one of Boise's most haunted houses once stood currently occupies the grounds of Boise's Carnegie library, built in 1905.

WHERE TO SEE IT: The approximate location of Jesse Black's haunted house can be visited at the site of Boise's Carnegie library, at 815 West Washington Street, between Eighth Street to the east and Ninth Street to the west. The house most likely would have been located somewhere on the east side of the library now occupied by the lawn across from St. Michael's Episcopal Church.

9
GHOSTS TRAVEL

THE HAUNTING OF THE BOISE LITTLE THEATER

When a person dies in a place they love, or when they die young, especially in a violent or tragic manner, their imprints, believers in paranormal activity claim, remain behind, tied to those locations. Some spirits, however, attach themselves to objects and items important to them. In the case of Boise's Little Theater, the structure itself became both the place and the object to which several entities have reportedly bound themselves, even after the theatrical troupe built a new theater in another location after the original playhouse burned down on May 16, 1956. The theater group started as the Boise Little Theater in February 1948, when a committee formed to organize a new acting troupe. The first productions included *Arsenic and Old Lace*, a tale of two "loveable old spinsters" who poison their suitors' elderberry wine with arsenic. These plays were performed on stages offered for use by Boise Junior College and the Veterans Administration auditorium, among others. Thankfully, the old theater at Gowen Field was made available in October 1948 for the specific use of the nascent acting troupe.

For eight years, the Boise Little Theater's thespians staged plays before increasingly large audiences as the public came to love the amateur acting collective. Two members of the group in 1956 were Justice Craycroft, a twenty-nine-year-old writer employed with KBOI Television, and George McKean, a forty-year-old airplane mechanic and the superintendent of Morrison Knudsen Company aircraft maintenance at its Boise Airport hangar. The two men also held important positions within the Boise Little

The Boise Little Theater's first location at Boise's Gowen Field in the 1940s. *Boise Little Theater Photo Collection.*

Theater organization, taking on roles such as, in Craycroft's case, assistant director, and for McKean, supervisor of stage furnishings. On May 16, 1956, the actors were performing the beginning act of their version of *The Fifth Season* at approximately 9:15 p.m. when fire began to spill out from behind the curtained background of the stage and climb the walls of the theater while actor Vaughn Price recited his lines. With nearly three hundred persons in the crowd, ushers stepped in and controlled the audience's natural inclination to panic, shepherding the entirety of the large group outside the theater in approximately thirty seconds. Sadly, both Craycroft and McKean were not included when a count was taken as the theater burned in a "roaring holocaust," as a writer for the *Idaho Statesman* described the catastrophe. McKean had been sitting in a row close to the stage when "flames exploded like roman candles through a stage door at the theater's south side," prompting him to jump on stage in an attempt to find his wife, also a member of the troupe. His body was found an hour after the fire started, lying just inside the southside stage doorway. Justice Craycroft was found lying in a small room near the theater's west entrance. Some

(Upper Left)
Back row—Matt Ellis, Harmon Barton, Bob Preece, Bill Snow.
Third row—Dale Blackburn, Millicent Daines, Ruth Dixon, Georgia Anderson, Bert Corkey.
Second row—Marian Shaw, Maurine Snarr, Beverly Behling, Marian Tillotsen, Norma Manning.
First row—Carma Hinchcliff, Bonnie Brian, Jeanne Binnie, Joan Scofield, Louann Huss.

(Lower Left)
Back row—Ray Herdti, Dale Brown, Alvin Rhodes.
Fourth row—Kay Randall, Ronald Ross, Harry Anderson.
Third row—Stanley Paul, Jack Critchlow, Arthalean Kay, Lorna Alvord.
Second row—Jeanette Dursteler, Isabell Lawrence, Neta Sullivan, Betty Jensen, Nadine Peterson.
First row—Orval Baggs, Mary Bingham, Virginia Bieler, Anna Mae Anderson.

(Above)
Back row—Kenyon Wilks, Howard Taylor, Justice Craycroft, Ken Willard.
Third row—Lila Presnell, Marian Hadlock, Beverly Batchelor.
Second row—Donna Farr, Arlene Sill, Kathleen Geffas, Virginia Porter.
First row—Shirley Reeder, Nancy McBride, Mary Lou Austin.

S E N I O R S

43

Justice Craycroft is the tallest man in the photograph, second man from the right in the back row. *U.S., School Yearbooks, 1880–2012; School Name: Ogden High School; Year: 1945. Ancestry.com.*

troupe members claimed he had been attempting to rescue the expensive furs the theater had borrowed from a local shop. Both men, the coroner later informed the public, died of suffocation before the flames reached them. Tragically, the organization lost two friends and important members of the troupe and, once again, found itself without a theater to call its own.

Thankfully, the citizens of Boise rallied around the actors, raising funds to erect a second theater in 1957. The City of Boise generously donated the land on which the theater sits. Architect and contractor Arthur Troutner designed the modernistic structure for free, and over $75,000 had been donated by the public to aid the Boise Little Theater in getting back to performing entertaining productions. On September 22, 1957, the theater opened its doors to its fans for the first time. Staff members had scrubbed the venue from top to bottom during "Operation Cleanup," as groups and volunteers dubbed the effort. The theater, it was made known, was a monument to the memories of Justice Craycroft and George McKean. Ten days later, on October 2, the group performed the play *High Tor* before a rapt audience. The Boise Little Theater has become the longest working playhouse in Idaho, still offering quality productions to this day.

The theater has hosted many happy spectators over the years, and quite a few of them have noticed residents of the supernatural kind making themselves known within the confines of this unique building. When the first strange occurrences began to take place is unknown, but the spirits of two men and a woman reportedly haunt specific locations in the venue.

The Boise Little Theater as it now appears. *Boise Little Theater.*

A possible identity behind the female entity is that of Margaret June Randolph, a member of the troupe in the late 1940s and early 1950s who moved to the Fort Worth, Texas area after 1951, where she passed away on June 6, 1961, at the age of thirty-nine from the effects of heart disease. There are no reports of a woman dying in the entrance lobby to the theater, where the female specter is said to haunt, nor in any other location in the building. She has been active at the front box office, frightening a few people out of their wits. One incident involving this spirit took place in the theater's ticket booth. A member of the staff was sitting in the small room with her dog with the door closed. The dog began to growl defensively, its fur standing on end and its ears back. The employee opened the door and looked into the empty theater, but her canine companion continued to growl and bark, staring at nothing her owner could see. The dog became more agitated. Now thoroughly spooked, the woman grabbed her pet, purse and coat and fled the building.

None of the ghosts are malicious in nature. They tend to play tricks, appear out of the corner of one's eye and even help at times. One example involves the four-year-old daughter of an actor rehearsing one evening with other members of the troupe. The little girl snuck away while the actors occupied themselves with rehearsal, making her way onto the stage and toward a trapdoor to the storage area below. The door in the floor had been left open by mistake. The child fell into the dark space below just as her mother realized she had accessed the stage. Members of the ensemble raced to the door below the stage and found it locked. The actors raced outside to the door accessing the basement of the theater and, on bursting into the room, found the girl standing below the trapdoor she had just fallen through approximately ten feet above, uninjured. When asked to describe what happened, the child replied, "Oh, the nice man caught me and put me down."

Additionally, belongings and props tend to disappear and reappear with some regularity, and lights turn on and off seemingly on their own. When Don Hawkins, theater director in the late 1990s, was working on a script one night after rehearsal, he experienced disembodied footsteps walking across the stage while he was looking directly at it from audience seating. Hawkins walked up on stage and distinctly felt that "someone was looking at me.... The hair went up on the back of my neck, and I just got out of there." Hawkins refused to be alone in the building from then on. One ghost favors the wardrobe room, where he messes with the lights during performances and, at times, appears in the small window that looks out onto the theater's breezeway. Staff leave on a lamp in the wardrobe room, where it sits beside a book on a small table. This is said to appease the ghost, who becomes irritated at times if disturbed by too much commotion or darkness.

The claims of paranormal activity eventually led to the members of Western Idaho Paranormal (WIP) being invited by theater staff to conduct a nighttime investigation of the entirety of the structure. The investigators experienced a range of activity, from shadows to auditory phenomena such as sighs, yawns and whispers, to a loud bang issuing from the building's lobby while the cameras of local television station KIVI filmed. WIP, an organization that has conducted hundreds of investigations of both commercial and residential cases, concluded that it had gathered strong evidence to support the claim that the Boise Little Theater was haunted and that the site left much more to be explored. Considering the sheer volume of reported experiences and stories of paranormal activity in the theater, it seems Boise's citizens, spectators and performers are not the only ones who love this theater.

WHERE TO SEE IT: The Boise Little Theater is hard to miss. It looks like a flying saucer made of lumber, brick and aggregate shingles. It is situated just north of Boise's new roundabout connecting Fort Street to Second and Third Streets to the south. Check out a show; you are sure to have a nice evening, and you might see a ghost as well.

10

BOISE EMBRACES SATAN

For the better part of three decades, an evil presence was felt by many Boise residents. Children had strange nightmares and began acting aggressively toward their parents. Teenagers began using drugs and engaging in self-mutilation while playing with Ouija Boards and Tarot Cards. Furthermore, they would draw strange symbols, fear going to church and show signs of multiple personalities. Strains of music by bands such as Metallica, Black Sabbath and Motörhead could be heard by parents, filling their children's minds to the brim with Satanic messaging while sinister groups of hooded figures were seen creeping around the Boise Foothills at night. Boise Police reported finding dead cats and dogs, used for ritual purposes, scattered all over the North End. It seemed that Satan had taken hold of the Boise Valley.

On Friday, August 18, 1972, a crowd of two thousand people gathered at Simplot Stadium in nearby Caldwell to hear speakers warn of the dangers facing society. Dr. John Wesley White addressed the crowd, telling them, "Satanic cults, witchcraft and 'devil worship' are becoming popular today—especially among many young people." The year before, a book called *The Exorcist* became popular in Boise. By the time the film adaptation was released three years later, hundreds of copies a month of the book were being sold in Boise bookstores. Around the same time, rumors of Satanic cults started to spread in Idaho. In the tiny town of Rathdrum, it was said that a coven of Satan-worshiping witches had abducted and murdered a young couple, Ronald and Rita Marcussen. Townspeople reported to police that they had encountered "human chains" of Satanists blocking roads near the town, and evidence of Satanic rituals were discovered in the woods. A rumor even began to circulate that Charles Manson, the cult leader whose followers were responsible for at least nine murders in California, wanted to move to Rathdrum because of the large concentration of witches there.

In the summer of 1975, rumors of Satanic cults moved closer to Boise after six cows were found dead and mutilated in rural Adams County, Idaho. Each animal's udders, tongue and sexual organ had been cut out, but the most startling aspect of this gruesome discovery was that no blood could be found at the scene of the crime. No mortal wounds were found on the cattle, leading police to believe they had been killed by poison darts or some other undetectable means. Similar cases of cattle mutilations had recently occurred in several other states, and each case was pinned on Satanic cults. When asked about the possibility that Satanists were responsible for the cattle mutilations, in this case, Adams County Sheriff Jim Hileman was quoted as saying: "I'm starting to lean toward it. I can't prove or disprove it. Anything is possible." As more mutalations were reported in Idaho through the rest of the decade, law enforcement decided to focus their investigations on these occult groups.

Evidence of Satanic rituals began to be found all around the Boise area. Police were called to the Quail Hollow Golf Course in North Boise, where a dead horse had been found. Similar to the cattle, this horse had been horribly mutilated. Its throat had been cut, not torn by an animal, and the inner organs had been removed. The horse's genitals were cut away "very neatly and very squarely," and very little blood was found at the scene. An investigator with the Ada County Sheriff's Office told the *Idaho Statesman* that the crime was likely related to the occult. The investigator also admitted that the sheriff's office had investigated several cat mutilations, also probably related to Satanists. At Jump Creek Falls, a popular weekend getaway spot southwest of Boise, a group of young men found a horrifying scene one Saturday morning. They were hiking above the main waterfall to find the fabled "Old Man of the Owyhees," a rock formation resembling a face. After climbing up out of the canyon, they stumbled upon what at first glance may have looked like a campsite. A ring of logs or rocks for sitting surrounded a fire pit, but as the men approached they saw something horrifying. A post had been sunk into the ground, and a dead animal was hanging from it. The corpse was assumed to be that of a goat with the head and hooves removed. Scattered around were pamphlets containing what looked like spells or incantations. The men felt an evil presence there and decided to abandon their hike.

As the people of Boise began hearing about evidence of Satanic activity around the Treasure Valley, other events around the state solidified fears that Satanists were hiding among the good people of Idaho. Thomas Eugene Creech was convicted in the 1974 double murder of a pair of hitchhikers. After picking them up near Boise, he drove them north to rural Valley County, where he shot both of them in the head. After being arrested in Glenns Ferry, Creech told police that he was a serial killer, a hitman for an outlaw biker gang and a Satanic priest. He claimed that forty-two people had died by his hand, many of them for occult rituals. Creech was sentenced to death and is currently the longest-serving resident on Idaho's death row. Another case of murder blamed on Satanism occurred in Blackfoot. When nine-year-old Zerick Winn was found dead in his bed, his mother, Kathi, was charged with his murder. Kathi killed her son by giving him a high dose of an antidepressant in his bedtime hot chocolate. She claimed a demon named Rahah had told her to kill Zerick. Kathi informed police that she had been raised in a Satanic cult that traveled the country. As a young girl, she had been married off to her stepfather, and her first child, Michael, had been sacrificed in a Satanic ritual when he was two months old. Kathi Winn is currently serving a life sentence for Zerick's murder at the Pocatello Women's Correctional Center. If not for her chronic mental health problems, she likely would have ended up on death row.

Another child death shocked not only the state but also the entire country. One chilly November evening, Robert Boesiger and his young son drove out to the Minidoka County Landfill near Rupert to help some teenagers pull their truck out of the mud. When Paul got his own truck stuck in the recovery attempt, he and his son started walking back to their home for more help. Passing the landfill, they spied an old metal drum. Robert's son looked inside first before Robert shined his flashlight inside the container and was horrified by what he thought he saw there. Instead of reacting to the gruesome sight, he got his son home and into bed before calling the police. When first responders did arrive, they confirmed Robert's fears. Inside the drum was the partially burned and mutilated body of an infant. Because there was no way to identify the body, when the coroner took possession of it, he wrote "Baby X" on his report. The autopsy indicated that Baby X was a three-week-old girl. Both of her hands had been cut off, her internal organs had been removed and she was possibly skinned. After she was placed in the drum, gasoline was poured on her and her body was burned.

It seemed pretty obvious to locals that Baby X was the victim of a Satanic ritual, and law enforcement did not seem too quick to try to discount the notion. At a press conference, the prosecuting attorney stated that he "couldn't rule out" the possibility that Baby X was killed by Satanists. Statements like this fueled rumors that Satanists were hiding among the citizens of the rural community. Letters and phone calls poured into local law enforcement about missing cats and men wearing dark robes. Most disturbing was a letter stating that women were being used as "breeders," being impregnated with babies for the express purpose of creating sacrifices.

Despite all of these leads, police could not uncover the murderers or even the identity of Baby X, so when an official from child protective services of San Bernardino, California, called, the police were ready to listen. A nine-year-old boy named Timothy came forward, telling adults that he had witnessed, and been the victim of, Satanic ritual abuse while his family had been living in Minidoka County. Timothy told his teachers, mental health counselors and police that he had been sexually and physically abused by Satanists. He said he was placed on a table with a Bible, and members of the cult gathered around to take turns abusing him while praying to the Devil. Timothy also told police and social workers he was forced to watch as babies were killed and burned as sacrifices to Satan, making some believe he had witnessed Baby X's death.

Officials in Boise began paying attention to these stories of ritualistic abuse from all over the country and Idaho. Detective Lieutenant Larry Jones of the Boise Police Department became increasingly concerned about the reports. He decided to take action by forming an organization called Cult Crime Impact Network (CCIN) as a way to help educate other law enforcement officers on how to recognize signs of ritual abuse. By 1989, the CCIN was publishing a bimonthly newsletter called *File 18*, which was sent out to over two thousand members of law enforcement, clergy and mental health professionals. Another Boise Police Detective working with the CCIN even went so far as to collect a file from the Idaho Historical Society containing information about the Satanic church run by inmates when the Old Pen was in operation. The CCIN partnered with a church organization in Boise called Dove Ministries. Together, the CCIN and Dove conducted several "deliverances" throughout the Treasure Valley. Jerry Lillibridge, a member of Dove's leadership board, told the *Idaho Statesman* that these ceremonies were similar to exorcisms. The practitioner would begin by talking to the possessed person, attempting to find out the name of the demon. Sometimes the victim would answer in an animalistic

A list of materials used by Satanists in their practice. *Old Idaho State Penitentiary Files.*

grunt or demon voice. Once the name was established, the entity would be cast out in the name of Jesus Christ.

One of the people helped by the Dove Ministries and CCIN was a young woman named Paula Olson. Like many teenagers in Boise, Paula had turned to Satanism as an escape from the difficulties of teenage life. Around the age of fifteen, she began listening to Satanic music, wearing black and drawing pentagrams on her school notebooks. Paula even believed that while playing with a Ouija Board with her friends she made contact with a deceased, high-ranking member of the Third Reich. She said that worshiping Satan made her feel powerful, but her mother and stepfather began to worry. They felt the need to lock their bedroom door at night after butcher knives were found under Paula's mattress. After Paula ran away a few times and was arrested for stealing from cars, her mother contacted the CCIN and spoke with Lieutenant Jones, but it was Paula who decided she needed help after a visit from a demon.

One night while listening to Satanic music, with incense and candles burning, Paula heard a noise outside of her bedroom window. Thinking it was a dog or someone walking by, she ignored it until it became a scratching sound on the window. Then she felt her bed move and watched in horror as the corner of the bed sank down. Paula closed her eyes for a time, scared to open them. When she finally did, she saw the creature sitting on the corner of her bed, cross-legged. Paula described it as half human and half werewolf, with small red eyes. It sat and stared at her for a time. Paula did not recount what made the demon leave, but that was the moment she decided to turn her life around and embrace the help offered by the Cult Crime Impact Network.

The CCIN became the go-to resource for media coverage of Satanism in Idaho. In July 1989, Jones was pictured on the front page of the *Idaho Statesman* in a bunker in the Boise Foothills near the Military Reserve Cemetery. The bunker was one of the places where Boise's Satanists went to conduct their dark rituals. Other places included Cottonwood Creek, Swan Falls, the desert around South Cole Road, Table Rock and its quarry. These places usually had fire pits and were covered in Satanic graffiti. Lieutenant Jones told the newspaper that dead dogs and house cats that had been skinned were found dumped in the hills north of Boise, implying that these animals had been used for Satanic rituals. He also pointed to graffiti in the bunker that read, "May your soul keep me young," as evidence of Satanic activity.

In the same article, Terry Clapp, a Boise psychologist, explained exactly how these Satanic cults got away with so many murders and sexual assaults. Clapp, who had been awarded a doctorate in psychology and a master's degree in theology, claimed that he treated many patients who had been victims of these cults. He said these sects could get away with what they were doing because many people in the community would deny there was a problem when confronted with facts, but also because cult leaders were very good at covering up their crimes. Clapp claimed cults would use alcohol, sex and drugs to attract young people into their groups. Most troubling was the way they disposed of the remains of their victims. They would burn the bodies until the bones were "of a consistency that allows them to be eaten by ritual participants." Clapp claimed that some of his patients had eaten the bones of their victims.

In a full-page story in the *Idaho Statesman* on January 5, 1992, "Caught in a Web of Cults," Lieutenant Jones was quoted as saying, "It is estimated that 50,000 to 60,000 ritual murders are committed each year in the country." The numbers were shocking, but they reinforced the need for Jones and his group's fight against Satanists. That same article ran an interview with a twenty-nine-year-old woman identified only as Ann. Ann testified before the Idaho Legislature in 1990 that her family was involved in up to twelve different covens in Idaho and that those covens were responsible for up to

750 murders. Jones went on to say in the same article that the bodies of victims are usually not found, because the cultists have figured out ways to dispose of them. Body parts unused in rituals were burned in homemade crematoriums, fed to dogs or dissolved in acid.

Dove Ministries was not the only religious organization that took notice of the increasing problem of Satanic ritual abuse. The Church of Jesus Christ of Latter-day Saints, or the Mormon Church, one of the predominant religions in Boise, was also aware of it. Elder Glen L. Pace was a member of the Presiding Bishopric and as such was one of the highest authorities in the church. On July 19, 1990, Elder Pace published a document that came to be known as the Pace Memorandum. In the document, he claimed to have examined sixty children of church members. After interviewing these kids, Pace came to the conclusion that many of them were sexually abused by Satanists who were also members of the Mormon Church. He also said that much of this abuse occurred within LDS meetinghouses or churches. Further, many of the abusers were temple recommend holders, a status that requires members to live the most upright of lives, supposedly abstaining from coffee, cigarettes and sexual sins. To obtain a temple recommendation, a member must be interviewed by their bishop, who has been given the power by God to determine whether or not someone is lying to him. The Pace Memorandum essentially says that children were being abused in Mormon churches by the people who were supposed to be acting most "God-like" and that church leadership was complicit in allowing the abuses to happen.

The panic over sexualized ritual abuse in the state led the Idaho Legislature to pass legislation to make the ritual abuse of children illegal. During the 1990 session, Idaho's lawmakers passed 18-1506A, "Ritualized Abuse of a Child." This law made it a felony if anyone "actually or in simulation, tortures, mutilates or sacrifices any warm-blooded animal or human being. Places a living child into a coffin or open grave containing a human corpse or remains. Unlawfully dissects, mutilates, or incinerates a human corpse." Many of these sections directly correlated to the mounting fears many parents had that Satanic cults lurked around every corner, ready to harm their children. The punishment for violations of any of the provisions of this law was life in prison. Despite existing for more than thirty years, this law has been applied only one time, to a man now in prison who thought he was doing "God's work," not that of the Dark Lord of the Underworld.

The fact that Idaho's ritual abuse law has not been used more frequently highlights the belief many experts have about the idea of Satanic cults committing murder and sexual abuse on a mass scale—that is, that the "crisis" was mostly made up. In 1994, Dr. Gale Goodman of the University of California–Davis conducted a survey of tens of thousands of police officers, prosecutors, social workers and psychologists. Of almost thirteen thousand allegations of ritual abuse, the survey found that not a single one could be corroborated. There was absolutely no evidence that Satanic cults were sexually abusing children or murdering anyone. Of course, there were cases perpetrated by individuals or couples Satanic in nature, but there was no indication that they were part of a larger movement. In fact, it seems that many of these cases were inspired by the constant rumors of Satanic cults and ritual abuse. In the survey's report, Dr. Goodman again put out a call for any evidence of cults, but to this day that call has not been answered.

Dr. Goodman's report helped bring about the end of the "Satanic Panic" in the United States. In Boise, many of the pieces of evidence that people like Lieutenant Jones presented were easily discredited. A week after the story on the bunker in the foothills was published, a young Boisean wrote in and claimed he wrote the "May your soul keep me young" graffiti. He said he was actually a Christian and the graffiti had nothing to do with Satan. In fact, he claimed the only things being sacrificed the night he wrote the message were hot dogs and marshmallows. Jones's claim that up to fifty thousand people a year were being killed by Satanists—with no evidence of any form to substantiate his claim—was ludicrous. Although he went on working for the Boise Police Department, the Cult Crime Impact Network filed its last annual report with the State of Idaho in October 1994, the same month Dr. Goodman's report was released.

Terry Clapp, the Boise psychologist who claimed that his patients were forced to eat bones, was also discredited. He faced at least six lawsuits from former clients, at least two of which claimed that Clapp worked hard to convince them their issues were caused by past sexual abuse by Satanic cults. As part of his therapy sessions, Clapp was conducting exorcisms in an attempt to rid his patients of their literal demons. He was also accused of having sex with one of his patients, claiming that God told him to make her his "spiritual wife." After hearing all of these complaints, the state pulled Clapp's license to practice psychology, although Idaho law still allowed him to practice as an unlicensed counselor.

The crimes that Idaho's public were convinced were committed by these Satanic cults were proven not to be. Rita and Ronald Marcussen of Rathdrum were not killed by witches; they were shot by a man who was trying to steal their car. That leaves Baby X, who was found mutilated and burned in a barrel. Authorities quickly discounted the possibility of Satanic ritual and offered a more feasible scenario. The child had in fact died of pneumonia, which was confirmed on the autopsy. It was likely that Baby X was part of a family of immigrant laborers who chose not to report the death for fear that authorities would check their legal status. Instead, they tried disposing of the body by burning it in the barrel, and what was left was predated on by animals. Cattle mutilation also can usually be explained by animal predation.

The Satanic Panic was considered to be the third great moral panic in the United States, after the Salem Witch Trials and the McCarthy hearings. It was marked by fear, misinformation and leaders who chose to use misinformation to stoke fear, often for their own benefit. True, there are real-life Satanists out there today, but they were not responsible for the murders and sexual abuse described in this chapter. They do not believe in a literal Satan but use the name as a metaphor. In fact, they preach empathy and compassion toward all. Unfortunately, Satanic panic has not completely gone away. Even as this book was being prepared to go to print, stories could be found in newspapers about politicians or high-profile religious leaders calling out musicians for "Satanic" performances at widely broadcasted events. As long as there is something to be afraid of in our society, some people will blame it on Satan instead of searching for solutions to real problems.

WHERE TO SEE IT: Wander around the Boise desert long enough and you'll see some kind of signs of activity that look Satanic in origin. You might even come across a bunker in the foothills full of "satanic" graffiti. Just be sure to use your critical thinking skills before proceeding.

11

WHAT'S THAT NOISE
IN THE BASEMENT?!

O n the southwest corner of the intersection of Leadville and Linden Streets looms a house that could easily be cast as the background in a horror film. Its yellowing stucco walls accentuate the deteriorating stone foundations, visual elements that lend validity to claims that the home is haunted. The building is known as the "Murder House," or the "Chop Chop House." The names fit. In short, the home as 805 Linden Street looks evil, a place where something truly horrible occurred, as it did on June 30, 1987. Yet, construction on 805 Linden began in 1910 and was completed in 1911, meaning seventy-six years of history had taken place before Preston Murr was shot in the shoulder and head in the basement of the grim-looking structure. Murr's murder serves to distract a perpetually interested public from the history of the building prior to June 1987 and the deaths that occurred there before that.

The original owner of the now infamous home was a construction contractor named Guy Matthews, a prominent figure in Boise during the time the home was constructed. Matthews built the home in the developing Ivywild area of South Boise, where the extension of the streetcar lines connected the new subdivision to downtown. After the home's completion, Matthews's family and various other families called the place home for a handful of years before the Bragunier family moved in around 1928. The Braguniers resided at 805 West Linden Street for over thirty years, raising kids there and, eventually, passing it down through the family to

The east side of the Boise Murder House at 805 West Linden Street. *Idahistory Photo Collection.*

Vera M. Collins, who started the Collanaire Nursing Home in the house. Several seniors being cared for at the facility ended up dying there in the 1950s. Birdie E. Sexton was Pearl Bragunier's mother. Birdie died on June 22, 1952, as a youthful ninety-one-year-old, shortly after the death of Pearl, who died at the age of seventy-two that same year. Ellen Lyndsey Marker also died at the Linden home, on July 10, 1959, at the age of eighty-nine. John Eggan had died in the home at the age of seventy-one in March 1958.

Well before the murder of Preston Murr in 1987, paranormal activity may have occurred at 805 West Linden due to the handful of deaths attached to the location from the time when it was an old folks home. In an article written by Michelle Heart for Boise radio station 107.9 Lite FM, a woman going by Kristi W. recalled a frightening memory of walking down Leadville Avenue when she lived in the area as a kid and seeing "a woman in an upstairs window banging on it." This is a strange thing to witness to be sure, but not paranormal in nature, until you consider that Kristi also described how eerie it was that the woman "was screaming but there were no sounds." Some of the elderly women who died at 805 West Linden were stricken with "senility," or dementia; for believers in the supernatural, it certainly seems possible that one of these confused and unfortunate women linger in the home even now.

Yet, the "Murder House"—the "Chop Chop House" to some—did not become infamous until June 30, 1987. At that time, middling drug dealer and convicted killer Daniel Rogers, along with his wife, called the then-decrepit building they owned home. Rogers had a personal history of mental health issues and crimes trailing him across several states, including South Carolina, Alabama, Florida and California. He molested an underage girl in South Carolina in the 1970s, abused his wife from a previous marriage, committed robbery, dealt drugs and even perpetrated the murder of George Weatherwax in California in 1977. Rogers pleaded guilty to second-degree murder and was sentenced to just five years behind bars. After serving his paltry sentence, Rogers moved to Boise about 1984 and eventually purchased the home at 805 West Linden, where he lived with his new wife, Kathryn. He had not been rehabilitated under the supervision of the California penal system.

From his home in South Boise, Rogers ran a middling drug operation and sold firearms. Preston Murr became one of his "clients" and associates,

Boise, Broadway facing north from the intersection with Sunset Road. *P3120, Idaho State Archives.*

purchasing marijuana from him, in about April 1987, Murr's sister Tonda Dykman-Streeper told reporters. However the relationship started, Murr and Rogers knew each other fairly well by Monday, June 29, 1987, the last full day of Murr's life. Eerily, Murr woke and drank with friends before the intoxicated group attended a funeral that morning. After the service, two men provoked a fight with Murr. After the brawl, he retreated to his sister's apartment, also in Southeast Boise near Bown Crossing, punched a wall and trashed the place, leaving smears of blood throughout the room. After cooling down, Murr received a call on his sister's line in which a threat against his life was made, prompting Murr to call the police to report the sinister call. Following the call to police, Murr rang Rogers in an attempt to discover who made the threatening call. After hanging up the phone, Murr left the apartment and walked to a nearby Circle K convenience store with a baseball bat in hand to meet Rogers.

When Rogers and his companion, thirty-one-year-old Daron Cox, arrived, they saw Murr on the pay phone outside the Circle K. Murr climbed in Rogers's vehicle, and the group returned to Murr's sister's place to discuss the possible whereabouts of some guns, drugs and money that had been stolen from Rogers. The three men left the apartment in the early evening and drove around Boise, stopping at several locations, never finding Rogers's stolen contraband. It may have been Rogers or Cox who called to threaten Murr, but in any case, after driving around aimlessly, the men went to 805 Linden Street around 10:00 p.m. to smoke a joint and discuss the situation. They entered the basement and, from what Daron Cox told police, began to fight.

Just after midnight on Tuesday, June 30, Clinton B. Sparks at 722 West Linden, across the street from Rogers's place, heard what sounded like running and shouting followed by the shadows of what appeared to be two men approaching his door. He heard a loud banging on his storm door and someone screaming desperately, "Let me go! Let me go!," before running off again. After things quieted down, Sparks opened the door and found a large quantity of blood smeared on it. He called the police and reported the incident, but perplexingly, the authorities never responded to the call. A transcript of the call highlights the alarming nature of the situation when, after the dispatcher asked Sparks what was wrong, he replied: "Uh, I don't know. A couple of guys came up and beat on the door and, uh, I went out and I went out and looked and there's some blood on the door it looks like." The dispatcher asked if the men had left and "can you see 'em down the street at all?" Sparks replied, "Uh, there looks like there's

722 Linden Street, the house Preston Murr ran to after escaping from the basement of 805 West Linden. *Idahistory Photo Collection.*

something going on in the house across the street." The dispatcher then asked if he wanted an officer to check on the situation. Sparks said "yes," but an officer never responded. Reviewing the call after the fact, it is clear that the two dispatchers failed to describe to officers the appropriate priority level of the call and also did not submit the request within the ten-minute wait and respond limit.

Prior to running from the home at midnight, Preston had been in the basement smoking a joint when an altercation broke out. At this point, based on trial testimony, Rogers shot Murr in the shoulder with a .357 Magnum revolver. Bleeding profusely, Murr ran as best he could up the steps and out the door across Linden Street, eventually making his way to 722 West Linden Street. Blood was found pooled and smeared about the neighborhood when police finally came to the crime scene on June 30, after Sparks called again at 8:00 a.m. Murr had eventually been caught by Rogers and Cox, then pulled back into the basement and shot in the back of the head by Rogers with his pistol. After Murr was murdered, Sparks witnessed Rogers and Cox hose off the front porch. Using a large knife and an axe, Rogers and Cox dismembered Murr's corpse, separating it into thirteen pieces that they then placed into trash bags, along with bloody rags, clothing and other pieces of their victim's belongings. They drove Rogers's wife's Grand Prix past Weiser, Idaho, to Brownlee Reservoir just outside of the town of Cambridge, where they sank the remains of Preston Murr. They placed several bags

89

A window looking into the basement of the Boise Murder House at 805 West Linden Street, where Preston Murr was executed and dismembered. *Idahistory Photo Collection.*

with body parts that would not sink on a bluff one hundred feet above the body of water. A bag full of rags and clothing was dumped into a trash bin in Meridian, Idaho. Rogers was arrested that morning after he arrived with his wife, Kathryn, to find the police swarming 805 West Linden Street, now the "Murder House."

Police had been issued a search warrant after finding blood trails and smears leading to 805 West Linden. In the basement, they found bullet fragments in the dryer, a bullet hole in the stairs and copious amounts of blood. They had no body to arrest Rogers for murder, but they did find thirteen pounds of marijuana. This gave police enough to arrest Rogers on charges of drug possession. Boise Detective Sergeant Jim Tibbs told reporters that police found blood throughout the bottom floor of the house leading to the basement. When Tibbs descended the stairs to the cellar, he described drips of blood on the steps. Of course, downstairs, he found more blood where the dismemberment of Murr took place. Daron Cox described to police prior to trial that the men used a board as a chopping block with the ax and knife, and he took police to the dumpster in Meridian where the knife and bloody bags from disposing of the body resided. Cox said Rogers threatened his family, saying to him that he is "either with me, or against me." Thus, a terribly frightened Cox, who had just seen Rogers shoot a man twice in cold blood, helped dismember and dispose of Murr's body. Cox was sentenced to five years in prison for aggravated assault and aiding in the commission of a felony. Based on the testimony of over fifty witnesses, Rogers was sentenced to life in prison. He is still serving his sentence ten miles south of Boise at the Idaho State Correctional Institution.

Rumors abound about the "Chop Chop House." A fraternity never called 805 West Linden Street their headquarters or witnessed blood dripping down the walls. Yet college students did rent rooms in the "Murder House" in the 1990s and 2000s; the house is rented to this day. In fact, it is presently owned by a cousin of Daniel Rogers. Most people who have lived in the home since 1987 and talked of their experiences described a feeling of utter repugnance and being ill at ease when in the basement. Whether they knew of the house's past prior to their experiences is not known, as most did not say. When 107.9 Lite FM requested past tenants share their stories in September 2021, they received quite a few replies. Some are truly chilling. A respondent calling himself "Dan D" shared that he and his girlfriend were lying in bed one evening as midnight neared when "we heard someone walk up the stairs. Didn't think much of it, thought it was a roommate, but then we heard it again and we never heard anyone go downstairs." Thinking they might be getting robbed, the couple went downstairs and outside in the front yard when they heard strange sounds.

Once outside, the two mortals found nothing out of sorts, so they stood on the porch to make it known they were home and that they suspected someone was creeping around. Dan described seeing shadows move in his peripheral vision until his companion "asked if I was seeing this stuff too?" At that point, Dan said he stepped out into the front yard and looked up into the front room with the big window off of Linden Street. He described seeing "a big black oily looking thing. I doubt what I'm seeing until it moves back towards the dresser, stops, and goes to the door" and disappears. Dan continued, describing witnessing "a mirror sitting next to the door on the porch" that caught his attention, and, as he looked in the mirror, seeing "a ball of oily darkness coming down the pillar." The ball filled up the space of the mirror and took form without the reflection, then passed through him, he said.

He shared that he never went back inside the house and that his friend "B" continued to live there a little longer. In parting, Dan asserted, "Feel free to doubt me and call me crazy, I don't care." Though others have reported strange sounds, shadows, figures and feeling horrible while in the house, Dan's account is the most eerie, yet is somewhat credible. Perhaps the spirits of those seniors who passed in the building when it was a nursing home linger, providing company to Preston Murr, a guy who just wanted to smoke a joint but ended up being murdered and dismembered by Daniel Rogers, a man already possessing a long and violent criminal record.

WHERE TO SEE IT: The Boise "Chop Chop House" is located at the intersection of Leadville and Linden Avenues, where it sits grimly watching cars go by as it slowly falls into decay. This is one haunted house that looks the part.

12
THE LOST SOULS OF FORT BOISE

Violence accompanied the nation's push westward from the start. Indeed, the conquest of the West would not have been possible without the repeated application of violent force. Boise City played its part in the epic that was westward expansion. Fort Boise was established between July 2, 1863, and July 4, 1863, to protect migrants trekking west, the gold supply from Confederate agents and eventually Native Americans from vengeful miners and settlers. The fort witnessed its fair share of deaths from accidents, murders, battlefield casualties, suicides and, most of all, disease. Soldiers received paltry salaries, which they too often spent on liquor and women. As a result, despondency, melancholia and anger were regularly displayed on the grounds of the garrison post. If the claims of many paranormal investigators are correct—that sadness and despair play a part in generating hauntings—then both the grounds and buildings of the old military post are good candidates for being haunted. Currently, the Fort Boise campus maintains two tenants, both government entities: the Veterans Administration Hospital and the City of Boise Department of Parks and Recreation.

Life at Fort Boise was one of routine followed by more routine. To be an enlisted man after the Civil War concluded in 1865 was not considered by society at large as a prestigious or honorable career. Many of the soldiers who found refuge on the frontier suffered from post-traumatic stress disorder as a result of their service during the war, and they frequently turned to the bottle or other drugs, such as opium, to quiet their haunting memories,

Boise, military posts, Boise Barracks, with a view of the 1910 hospital and tuberculosis ward. *P1986-10-11, Idaho State Archives.*

nerves and anxieties. Others were lonely, as life in the West could be isolating, despite the seeming abundance of space offered by the plains, deserts and sage lands that frequently served as a backdrop for their time as soldiers. The blowing of the wind often became a troubling foe to many forlorn troopers. This was true of the men living and working at Fort Boise and the military post's support camps in the surrounding territory. Suicide plagued most frontier military commands.

Many soldiers died in combat fighting the "Snake Indians," as the Shoshone, Bannock and Northern Paiute were commonly referred to in the 1860s. Others met their end in combat against the Nez Perce in 1877, the Bannock in 1878 and the Sheepeaters (the last remaining group of Shoshone) in the mountains of Central Idaho in 1879. But most soldiers died of disease. Of the many maladies that threatened a trooper on the frontier, consumption—tuberculosis, as we call it today—proved one of the most prolific. Those afflicted with the illness developed lesions in their lungs, less frequently in their spine or brain, and occasionally on their faces and other extremities, that quite literally consumed them. Other diseases included ailments brought on by the undercooking of food or the transmission of bacteria from fecal matter on a person's hands or in the water consumed by an individual. Cholera, dysentery and typhoid fever, among others, were spread in such a manner. Typhus was transferred to humans by bacteria carried by rats and possums, while diphtheria bacteria could be caught by mist or spray when a person with the bacterial infection coughed or when someone handled rags or tissues used by infected persons. These contagions entered their victims, then ravaged them, turning the sufferers of such afflictions into specters of who they once had been. Diphtheria formed a gray bacterial buildup at the top of a person's throat while their glands swelled and fever set in. The infected person literally choked to death. Crude tracheostomies were the only chance—a slim one at that—to save the infected, more often than not children.

The sad story of the family of Brevet Major Patrick Collins, the commander of Fort Boise for much of the 1870s, illustrates the tragedies that often decimated families and bands of soldiers in the nineteenth-century West. As early as 1865, the Collins family had lost a young son, Daniel, who died on November 23 at fifteen months old. Daniel's ailment remained unnamed. Major Collins continued to fight the Shoshone, Cayuse and Paiute in 1866, but he was called away from Boise City to fight the Apache in Arizona in 1869. The major was no stranger to death, having fought in some of the most brutal combat experienced by the Army of the Potomac during the Civil War, including the Battle of Second Bull Run in late August 1862 and Antietam on September 17, 1862. The major returned to Boise in 1876. He was involved in the campaign against the Nez Perce in 1877 and in the Bannock War of 1878. He continued to fight after the greatest tragedy of his life occurred, the death of four of his sons at the hands of scarlet fever at Fort Boise between January 8 and January 14, 1877.

As the commander of the post, Major Collins lived in the commander's quarters, along with his family. It is one of the oldest buildings to currently occupy the grounds of Fort Boise, or Boise City for that matter, having been constructed in 1863. In January 1877, staff for the *Idaho Daily Statesman* described the scene within the house: "We were present in this house of mourning on Sunday, where we saw little Wlllie [*sic*] who seemed as if calmly sleeping; but the angel of death had summoned the gentle spirit away a few hours before." Three other Collins children died in the commander's quarters. Mrs. Collins and another child, Carrie, age ten, pulled through. The major continued in his role as commander of Fort Boise, but an accident involving a few spooked horses and an ambulance wagon led to his own death on November 11, 1879, near where the Cottonwood Creek flume crosses Mountain Cove Road. Two other men rode in the wagon, Colonel John Green and W.W. Calkins, and when the

Patrick Collins in the 1860s. *MS 730, Idaho State Archives.*

horses began to gallop up the hill toward officer's row, they jumped from the wagon and sustained no serious injury. But Major Collins hit his head on a rock, leading to a serious concussion that claimed his life a short time later at the fort hospital. After so much tragedy, Mrs. Collins packed up her remaining three children and left for Cincinnati, Ohio.

The commander's quarters sits next to the officer's quarters, also known as the captain's quarters, a building constructed in 1909–10 on the same spot as the previous officer's barracks. This building is reported to possess several hauntings, one involving the supposed apparition of an adolescent girl playing outside the building, wearing a pleated dress and knee socks and with long brown hair. The families of officers often lived with them, and like the four fever-stricken boys of Major Collins, some died while they lived at the post, either at their home quarters or at the fort hospital just down the hill. Either way, the ghost of a child outside the officer's quarters

The commander's quarters at Fort Boise, built in 1863–64. *Idahistory Photo Collection.*

Boise, Idaho military posts, Fort Boise Post Hospital. *P1977-180-2m, National Archives General Services Administration Photography Collection. Idaho State Archives.*

The grave of Major Patrick Collins and his sons at the Fort Boise Military Cemetery. *IdaHistory Photo Collection.*

adds up—to believers, that is. Some candidates for such a specter do in fact exist. On November 28, 1886, Maud G. Andrus, wife of Lieutenant Frank Andrus, died, as did the couple's young daughter. Maud's illness, noted her obituary in the *Idaho Daily Statesman*, had not been unexpected, as she had been ill for several weeks. Additionally, the death notice mentioned that her service would take place at the Boise Barracks; her home would have been the officer's quarters. Maud was twenty-two years old; her daughter's age was not mentioned.

Two soldiers also haunt the upper reaches of the building, standing at the top of the stairs looking down at the frightened mortals below. Doors are said to creak and have been seen to open and close on their own, whispers

The Fort Boise Officer's Quarters was constructed in 1910. *IdaHistory Photo Collection.*

Boise military posts, Fort Boise. Army officers with their families at the fort. *P1976-138-50, Idaho State Archives.*

emanate from empty rooms and footsteps can be heard in unoccupied wings of the large building. A few officers did die at the post, including a Captain Yates, who was thrown from his mount while running down one of his soldier's horses on the garrison drill field in 1906. The stricken officer died sixteen hours later at the post hospital. Perhaps Yates returned to his quarters and never left.

Most of the deaths at Fort Boise occurred at the post hospital, both the original structure and the building now on the site, built in 1910 on the same location. Soldiers and citizens died at the post infirmary of disease more often than not, though freak accidents also took place. On September 13, 1897, for example, the healthy and robust Private Edward A. Cummings, generally a strong worker who hauled and stacked sixteen-pound cannonballs and served as a pitcher for the post baseball team, doubled over in pain and was taken to the fort hospital. He died of a ruptured vein in his intestines the same day. Another example of how death might strike from seemingly nowhere occurred when Annie M. Scott came to visit her brother-in-law, the hospital steward Charles W.R. Vanradasky, and her sister in June 1891. After weeks spent enjoying a pleasurable visit, on the morning of July 7, Annie woke up healthy and happy before turning considerably ill after lunch. The twenty-one-year-old woman passed away at the barracks infirmary that very day.

More violent deaths also occurred at the fort, as when troopers shot their fellow soldiers on accident, for example. Private John L. Allen died on Tuesday, September 30, 1885, when he was shot by a Sergeant Auring at the post firing range at approximately 2:00 p.m. Allen had peeked out from behind the wooden buffer at the end of the range, thinking the sergeant had concluded his firing. But as Allen started to replace the hole-filled target, Auring shot and struck the exposed man in the stomach. He died an hour later at the post hospital. Sometimes, things got a bit out of hand as well, such as when Corporal Thomas E. Shea died from gunshot wounds received when the post guard pursued an inebriated Shea after he escaped from the guardhouse, where he had been "a long time confined," as the deceased man's December 27, 1865 obituary put it. Somehow the prisoner got his hands on some liquor and some guns; he put the guns to

Boise, Idaho military posts, Fort Boise storehouse, granary and commissary office. *P1977-180-2g, Idaho State Archives.*

good use, shooting his way out of the jail. But when he was ordered to drop his firearms, Shea refused with intense emotion and was shot.

Suicides also tragically occurred with some regularity at Fort Boise. Some men ended their lives while intoxicated and were thus more susceptible to the sadness they carried with them, such as when Private Michael Healey shot himself in the heart with his carbine on Tuesday, October 14, 1879. His obituary read, "He was esteemed in the company as a good soldier and a good man, but subject to fits of depression after being on a spree," and that "he had lately been indulging in one of his occasional sprees, and while recovering from its effects committed the rash deed." Another victim by their own hand was Private Patrick Grant, a cavalry man who shot himself with a revolver in the right side of the head, the ball exiting through his left shoulder, while in the field near Salubria, Idaho, in early July 1881. It was agreed that "depression of the mind, caused by unknown reasons…occasioned the rash act." Grant died at the post hospital on or around July 7, 1881.

Yet another tragedy occurred at the end of a rope when Sergeant Oliver Plunkett hanged himself from the pulley of the loading and unloading area in the commissary building on November 28, 1897. Again, whiskey was said to have aided the despondent man in committing the desperate act. A signed confession on a slip of paper was located in Plunkett's pocket. It was said that "despondence due to drink during the past week was the cause of the act." As Commissary Sergeant, it had been imperative that Plunkett maintain sobriety, a state he maintained since he arrived at the Boise Barracks on February 16, 1896. It had been only the week prior that anyone noticed he had been drinking heavily and the cause of this sudden dereliction of duty could only be guessed at. He left behind two children, a ten-day-old baby and his wife.

Other than the officer's quarters, the only regularly reported haunted building at the fort is the hospital, which later served as a tuberculosis and mustard gas ward. It was constructed on the spot of two previous infirmaries in 1910. The building consisted of several barracks with beds. Nurses tended to the sick men, bringing them what comfort they could. It also housed kitchens, doctor's offices, warm water bathing rooms, bathrooms and, ominously, a "dead room" on the bottom floor. While men did not die at drastic rates in the ward, a handful did. When one also includes those who passed away at the previous hospitals on the site, it is not surprising the building is reportedly haunted. Wasting away from tuberculosis, which veteran Harry H. McKendrick died of on March

The 1910 Boise Barracks hospital and tuberculosis ward. *IdaHistory Photo Collection.*

24, 1920, or from the effects of mustard gas inhaled on the western front during the First World War, must have been torturous ordeals to endure. It is claimed that painful deaths such as these lead to the haunting of sites where extreme suffering occurred. Most recently, the facility was the headquarters of the Boise School District's Mountain Cove School until 2018, when the building was sold. Students and faculty alike spoke of eerie sounds and footsteps heard when no one else was around. In addition, doors closed seemingly by themselves. One staff member, used to working both early and late hours, described to the *Idaho Statesman* how "you could swear you could hear doors opening and closing, water running…we had a custodian years ago who refused to come in the building by himself, because he swore this building is haunted." With so many individuals having died at the site, it certainly fits the bill of a haunted old hospital and schoolhouse.

Lastly, the most haunted location tied to the old military fort is the Fort Boise Military Cemetery, farther up Boise's Mountain Cove Road, one of the city's easily accessible gateways to the Boise Foothills north of town. The cemetery was literally displaced starting in 1907, when it was decided that a new firing range would be more useful in the location occupied by the soldiers' and citizens' cemeteries. The site had been established as the main burial ground for early Boise City in 1863, when the first deaths, military or civilian, began to occur. Cottonwood Creek often flooded, inundating the four separate graveyards—for soldiers, civilians, Catholics and the town's Jewish population—with torrents of mountain water. A Dr. McInteeny, who died in 1866, reportedly went missing after a most severe flood in 1888. Even after a stone flume was constructed to redirect the troublesome creek in 1884, the area continued to flood. The area where dog and bike parks are located today was once the site of Fort Boise's original cemetery. Perhaps, in uprooting the dead, the mortal world upset the division between the living and the dead, causing the current military cemetery to be one of the most haunted locations in Boise, or Idaho, for that matter.

Confined within the rod-iron fencing of the military cemetery are many who experienced some of the most tumultuous times in American history. Several veterans buried there fought in the Mexican-American War in the 1840s, while others fought in the Civil War at major battles such as Bull Run, Second Bull Run, Antietam, Fredericksburg, Chancellorsville, the Wilderness and Gettysburg. Men like Sergeant Peter Vogel served in such times, only to be shot down in a brothel near the intersection of Eighth and Main in 1869. Others, like "Pony" Lawrence, died at the barrel of a gun in disputes over hay distribution. Pony was at the violence-plagued "Nine-Mile Junction House" east of Boise City, down the Boise River approximately

The view from the Military Reserve Cemetery looking toward Cottonwood Creek. It is here that Major Patrick Collins and his sons lie buried. *70-66.9, Idaho State Archives.*

where the town of Eagle is currently located. A few women who endured the frontier and died of disease—and a few by violence—rest in this place, as do their children, all having seen too few days among the living. Many died while engaged in the "Indian Wars" against tribes displaced by America's push westward, peoples such as the Shoshone, Paiute, Cayuse and Nez Perce. Some of the residents of the cemetery served in the Spanish-American War, during the Boxer Rebellion or in the Philippine Revolution. Among the activity at the site are reports of a child sitting on the bench near the north entrance of the cemetery by the old stone plinth monument dedicated, in part, to Sergeant Peter Vogel. In addition, large orbs are seen dancing about the place in "unnatural" patterns, and a tree seems to move outside the iron fence at one moment and then inside the next. Shadows are said to dart from one headstone to another, the apparition of a soldier is sometimes seen near the flagpole above the burial ground and disembodied voices float about the wind—some even caught on audio recordings.

Including the cemetery, Fort Boise is one of Idaho's most haunted places. Though the majority of supernatural experiences are reported in the officer's quarters, the old tuberculosis ward and the fort cemetery, orbs are also said to fly around the old parade grounds. With all the tragedy that took place on the grounds and in the buildings—both those still standing and those long demolished—other paranormal activity likely occurs on the property. It just has yet to be recorded.

WHERE TO SEE IT: Fort Boise's main entrance is located at the northern end of Fifth Street where it runs into Fort Street. The old guardhouse is easily discernible with its antiquated design, in contrast to the modern Veteran's Administration building looming behind it. The road leading from the main entrance takes visitors up to the ridge on which officer's row stands before descending into the flats once again. For those looking for the old hospital, it is located southeast of officer's row, nestled against the Cottonwood Creek Flume and Mountain Cove Road.

13

PROJECT GRUDGE

UNIDENTIFIED FLYING OBJECTS OVER THE BOISE VALLEY

On May 13, 1949, around 11:00 a.m., Robert Smith was driving from Caldwell to Boise along Highway 20. When he looked to his left, he saw a silvery object flying through the sky. The single object disappeared, then five more like it appeared, flying in a V-shaped formation over Shafer Butte. The objects began what Smith described as a "spiral letdown," a letdown being the slow, controlled reduction of speed and altitude when an aircraft is preparing to land. The formation dropped about four thousand feet, shot back up and then began another letdown. This time, though, the objects shot upward at a seemingly impossible speed and disappeared.

The whole ordeal lasted a little less than five minutes but gave Smith ample observation time. They left no vapor trail or exhaust, and there was no sound or odor left behind by the objects. They were half-circle shaped, with the leading edge coming to a point. The bottoms were dark, and the tops were shiny. No fins, antennae, rods, canopies or other projections adorned the craft; they appeared completely smooth. The objects were not connected physically, but moved in perfect formation, as if connected by an unseen force. The same day the sighting took place, Smith wrote a letter to the commanding officer at Wright Army Airfield (which had actually been renamed Wright-Patterson Air Force Base the year before) in Dayton, Ohio. Wright-Patterson was the home of the Air Material Command, which had been given responsibility to carry out Project Grudge from February to December 1949. Like Project Sign the year before, Grudge's mission was to gather and evaluate data from sightings of "flying saucers" all over the country.

On June 10, 1949, Special Agent Joseph Earl Kuttler arrived in Boise with orders to gather more information on Smith's sighting. Kuttler's first stop was the Yates Building, located at Ninth and Main. In room 442, he found the director of the Idaho Board of Publicity. That man told Kuttler that Robert Smith was a former writer for the Board of Publicity but had since taken a job in Lewiston, Idaho, with the *Lewiston Tribune*. The director suggested that Kuttler speak with the *Idaho Daily Statesman* reporter who had broken the story of the sighting. When Agent Kuttler arrived at the *Statesman*'s office, he made contact with that reporter. The next day, Kuttler and the *Statesman* reporter went to the place where Smith said the sighting occurred. It was about ten miles east of Caldwell and thirteen miles west of Boise on Highway 20. Agent Kuttler took some photos of the area and interviewed a nearby farmer, who said he had not seen a thing.

The reporter also told Agent Kuttler about a man named Kenneth Arnold, a Boise businessman, inventor and pilot. While flying his small plane near Mount Rainier in Washington State on June 24, 1947, Arnold spotted some objects in the sky. His description of these unidentified objects

The approximate location where Robert Smith had his flying craft sighting. The *X* indicates the location of Shafer Butte. *Special Agent Kuttler, Project Grudge, USAF.*

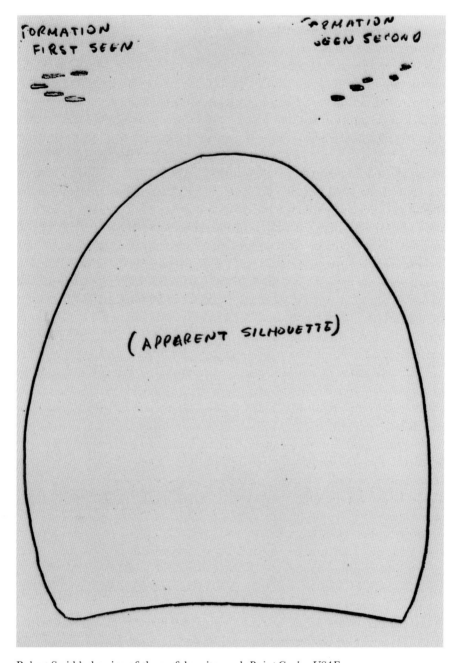

FORMATION
FIRST SEEN

FORMATION
SEEN SECOND

(APPARENT SILHOUETTE)

Robert Smith's drawing of the craft he witnessed. *Project Grudge, USAF.*

to an Oregon newspaper helped spawn the term *flying saucer*. Arnold later claimed that he did not describe his UFOs as looking like a saucer, only that they moved through the air like a saucer would move if you skipped one across the water. Back in Boise, Agent Kuttler attempted to make contact with Arnold but met with negative results, as Arnold was often out of town on business during this time. It's not noted why Kuttler wanted to speak with Arnold, as Arnold had already been thoroughly interrogated by the U.S. Air Force. Arnold's report ushered in the first great era of UFO reports in the United States, with sightings taking place in almost every state. With the start of the Cold War, the government had an interest in finding out the identity of objects flying through the nation's skies. The Air Force was given the responsibility to investigate these matters, and Project Sign was created in 1948. Project Grudge followed in 1949.

Joseph Earl Kuttler was probably the best Special Agent for this particular job, as he was an Idahoan himself. He was born in Saint Anthony and attended school in Pocatello. Kuttler joined the U.S. Army in 1941 in the quartermaster's corps and then became a member of the U.S. Air Force when it was created in 1947, rising to the rank of Major. While serving our country, Kuttler attended law school and was admitted to the bar in 1955. He opened a law office in Colorado Springs. When he was sixty-three years old, he realized that he had been an alcoholic all of his life and, in 2004, published a book about his time in recovery. Joe Kuttler passed away in 2013.

Special Agent Kuttler went to Gowen Field to check flight logs from May 13, the day Robert Smith sighted his UFOs above Shafer Butte. There were no military flights that day, except for a single F-51 on a test flight. Checking the flight path, Kuttler found that it had flown nowhere near where Smith said he saw the flying discs. No radar anomalies were recorded that day. A few commercial flights had occurred in the area, as well as some intermittent student flights from local airports, but Agent Kuttler determined that none of these would have been within Smith's line of sight. Finally, he verified with local law enforcement that Robert Smith did not have a criminal record. Additionally, Smith would have been a good judge of the distance and altitude; he flew B-24 bombers during World War II and was, at the time of his sighting, a first lieutenant in the U.S. Air Force Reserve.

The next day, June 11, 1949, Agent Kuttler arrived in Lewiston and made contact with Smith. After speaking with Smith, Kuttler determined that he was of above-average intelligence. Smith did not smoke dope or drink

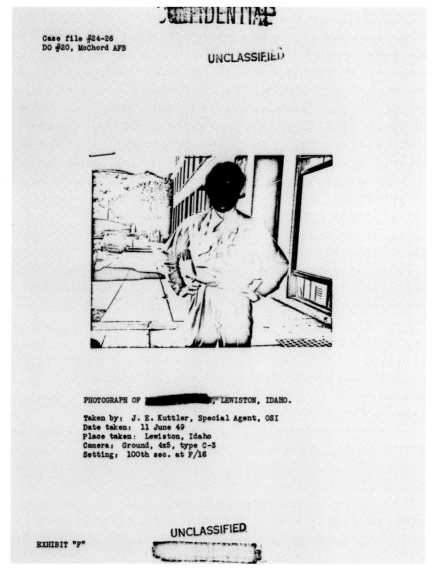

Robert Smith, face redacted. *Photo by Special Agent Kuttler, Project Grudge, USAF.*

to excess. These facts were verified by his employer, the editor in chief of the *Lewiston Tribune*, who considered Smith a "trustworthy and honorable employee." Agent Kuttler and others included the names of people they interviewed in their reports, but these names were in most cases redacted when released to the public.

Agent Kuttler next met with a man whose name was redacted in the report, a pilot instructor and trainer from Bradley Field, an airport that existed from 1954 to 1973 on Highway 20, approximately three miles northwest of Boise. This man reported that on April 24, 1949, he was flying from Bradley Field to Mountain Home in a L-13-B, a light aircraft, with two passengers on board. He was flying at nine thousand feet and traveling at 140 miles per hour. When he was about ten miles north of Mountain Home, the man observed what at first he thought to be a flock of birds flying about one thousand feet above him. The pilot and passengers, one of whom was a fellow pilot working out of Bradley Field, realized that these were some kind of aircraft, but none that any of them could identify. These crafts were described as oval-shaped, coming to a point in the forward sections of the objects. The pilot did not initially report this incident because of a couple of hoax reports in the area.

When he had gathered all the information he could, Agent Kuttler returned to Wright-Patterson Air Force Base and filed his report, released later as Project Grudge Report no. 319. As this report worked its way through the bureaucracy, two more sightings by seemingly reputable observers were made in the Boise area.

On July 24, another pilot, known only as Clark (his last name was left unredacted three times in this report) was flying a Piper Clipper from Ogden, Utah, to Nampa. Clark was approximately ten miles west of Mountain Home, near where the Bradley Field pilot made his sighting of multiple UFOs three months before. Clark was flying at around ten thousand feet when he saw seven objects come up on his left approximately five hundred feet below him. The craft were flying in formation, in two lines of three, with the seventh object slightly behind and above the rest.

As he watched, the unknown craft passed his plane and turned sharply to the right about 1,500 feet in front of him. The formation turned right again, and Clark thought they meant to ram him, but they flew past the right side of his plane. The crafts' turns were not slow, banking turns like earthly aircraft would make, but sudden and seemingly impossible. When they passed, Clark turned his own aircraft in the same direction in an attempt to keep them in sight. The formation was moving around 450 miles an hour and quickly disappeared from view.

The description of the craft in this case was fairly consistent with both Robert Smith's and that of the pilot from Bradley Field. Clark described them as being black and white, but shades of the colors he had never seen before and could not adequately describe. They were delta-shaped with no protrusions, and they were larger than a fighter plane. While still in the air, Clark called Boise Radio at Gowen Field and asked if any other aircraft were in the area. Boise Radio checked with radar stations at McChord and Hill Air Force Bases and discovered that no other aircraft were present at the time, a fact later verified by the Office of Special Investigations (OSI) Special Agent during his investigation.

Clark reported that after getting back on course, he noticed the engine in his aircraft ran much rougher than it had before the UFOs passed him, a strange occurrence considering the aircraft and engine were both brand new. When he landed at Nampa, he had the field mechanic examine the engine. The mechanic found that the spark plugs and wires had shorted and burned out. Clark retrieved seven of the eight spark plugs and turned them over to the investigator. The plugs and wires were sent to Wright-Patterson for analysis. Strangely, the study revealed that the spark plugs were completely serviceable.

The investigator in this case believed that Clark was a reliable witness. He had a good reputation and perfect eyesight. Clark had logged almost fourteen thousand flight hours in the twenty-one years he had been a pilot. During World War II, he trained pilots for the Army and Navy and also spent decades teaching civilians to fly. This incident became Project Grudge Report no. 410.

The final Treasure Valley UFO sighting of the Project Grudge era was on July 30, 1949. A biologist employed by the Idaho Department of Fish and Game, whose name was redacted, was traveling east between Nampa and Boise on Highway 30 (now I-84). About six miles from Nampa, and driving slowly, the biologist was looking for pheasants in the field to the south of the road when a glint in the sky drew his attention. He described the object as "brilliant," delta-shaped, metallic and of a bluish color he had never seen before. This object was about forty-five degrees from the ground, eight hundred to one thousand feet in elevation and traveling very fast, eight hundred miles per hour, Mr. Redacted estimated. He watched the object, which was initially traveling west, make a U-turn and gain elevation as it started heading east toward Boise, where it quickly left the biologist's sight. This man was also a trained pilot.

This sighting was reported to Mountain Home Air Force Base but assigned to an OSI investigator from Hill Air Force Base in Utah. The investigator did not go into the same amount of detail that Agent Kuttler had, seemingly only interviewing the witness and not checking for other aircraft in the area at the time. Project Grudge ended in December 1949, but its more famous little brother, Project Blue Book, picked up where Grudge left off and ran until 1969. Projects Sign, Grudge and Blue Book investigated hundreds of sightings of unidentified flying objects and generated some six hundred thousand pages of documentation, papers now housed in the National Archives. A few of these incidents can be written off as mundane events, but most were left unexplained by the U.S. Government. Since then, Boise has been known as a "UFO hot spot," with several sightings reported in the area every year.

So what were these "flying saucers" that were spotted by several reliable witnesses in the Boise Valley in 1949? Theories are put forth that they were alien spaceships, experimental aircraft, products of mass hysteria brought on by early Cold War fears or just clever hoaxes. Whatever it was, something was haunting the skies over the Treasure Valley in the summer of 1949. Perhaps someday we will learn what these things were, but until then, we hold out hope that the truth really is out there.

WHERE TO SEE IT: As you go about your day—and night—watch the skies over Boise and keep wanting to believe.

BIBLIOGRAPHY

1. The Blue Lady of the Midway Saloon

Boise City Directory. Boise, Idaho.
Idaho Statesman (Boise, ID). "Echo of Saloon Days." April 14, 1916, 7.
———. "Ended Life with Carbolic Acid." February 1, 1906, 5.
———. "Ghost Failed to Appear at Usual Hour." January 22, 1916, 6.
———. "Ghost of Woman Hangs around Former Saloon." January 20, 1916, 5.
———. "'Rover' Faces the Extreme Penalty." January 16, 1916, 7.
———. "'Rover' Finds a Home Near Murphy, Ida." January 21, 1916, 7.

2. The Ghost of Poor Little Clare Church

Burrows, Ken. "Ghost in a Boise Home." *Idaho Statesman*, September 23, 1973.
Idaho Statesman. "Funeral." July 20, 1905, 5.
———. "He Drank Poison." July 18, 1905, 5.

3. Ghost in the Cell

Behind Gray Walls Podcast. "EP 21—Phillips and Hastings." March 24, 2020.
Idaho Inmate Prison Records "Hastings, Raymond Kenneth-8330."

Idaho Statesman. "Charges Filed against Trio in Shooting." September 9, 1951, 9.

———. "Convicted Slayers Accused in Prison Break Attempt." June 23, 1953, 1.

———. "Court Rejects Doomed Man's New Trial Bid." December 29, 1951, 2.

———. "Death Charged Men Review Fatal Holdup." November 30, 1951, 5.

———. "Escapes Guard on Boise Street." September 9, 1954, 1, 6.

———. "FBI Tentatively Identifies Skeleton Found at Arco." January 24, 1969, 6

———. "Idaho Manhunt Spreads over 1,000-Square-Mile Area." September 25, 1954, 5.

———. "Sentences Commuted for Slayers." January 28, 1953, 1.

———. "Two Gunmen Jailed in Shooting of Boise Grocer." September 8, 1951, 1.

4. A Miner, a Frat and a Ghost or Two: The Storied Past of 110 Main Street

Idaho Daily Statesman (Boise, ID). "Attends Frank Galey." January 27, 1930, 7.

———. "Bullet Kills Boise Girl, Maribel Galey, 13, Dies after Accident with .22 Pistol." May 6, 1942, 1.

———. "Many Attend Galey Funeral." May 8, 1943, 3.

Idaho Statesman. "Kappa Sigs Plan Nov. 2 Move-in, Pioneer Regan Home Leased by Fraternity." October 23, 1969, 11.

———. "Moving Day on Main Street, Kappa Sigmas Take Over Historic Boise Home." November 9, 1969, 75.

Idaho Sunday Statesman. "Sells Home." September 17, 1939, 6.

Parnell, Dusty. "Historic Home on Main Street Full of History." *Idaho Statesman*, February 23, 2013.

Penson, Betty. "What's behind Those White Pillars? Biography of an Historic Fraternity House." *The Idaho*

State of Idaho. "Certificate of Death: Timothy Regan." Board of Health, Bureau of Vital Statistics, Reg. Dist. No. 292, File No. 27698. Filed October 9, 1919.

Sunday Statesman (Boise, ID), November 9, 1969, 14-B.

5. Lost Souls of the Idanha

Hart, Arthur. "Idaho history: Boise's Castle-Like Idanha Hotel Ushered in 20th Century." *Idaho Statesman*, April 9, 2016.

Idaho Daily Statesman. "First Plot to Kill Steunenberg. Orchard Planned To." March 25, 1906, 3.

———. "Hedges Arraigned in Court. Charged with Assault." June 25, 1907, 5. .

———. "Inquest in Goodbub Case. Coroner's Jury Decides." October 15, 1908, 3.

———. "Joseph V. Sweetman." September 19, 1919, 7.

———. "Jury Holds Jacobs Died by Own Hand in Leap To." May 19, 1921, 7.

———. "Kuna Farmer in Leap to Death Takes Own Life." May 18, 1921, 3.

———. "Mortuary Notice." July 17, 1905, 3.

———. "Pays Tribute to Sacrifice for Country Impressive." August 12, 1918, 5.

———. "Sudden Death of Chicago Man. Edward L. Juneau." November 18, 1909, 8.

———. "War Drives Girl Mad. Former Boise Girl Jumps off." October 11, 1914, 2.

———. "Well-Known Hotel Man Answers Last Summons Elmer." May 20, 1911, 2.

Idaho Statesman "Coincidence in Timing Cost Boisean His Life." May 2, 1975, 31.

———. "Idanha Hotel Shooting Kills 2." April 30, 1975, 44.

———. "Psychiatrists Explain Problems, Murder-Suicide Prevention Doubted." March 9, 1976, 1.

———. "We're Not Alone from Idanha Hotel to Hills above the Salmon [*sic*] River, Boise Brims with Real-Life Ghost Stories." October 31, 1997.

Ogden (UT) Standard-Examiner. "Shotgun Fire Kills Two in Hotel Hallway." April 30, 1975, 17.

Renk, Thomas B. *National Register of Historic Places Nomination: Idanha Hotel, Ada County, Idaho.* Boise, ID: Idaho State Historical Society, 1974.

Spokesman-Review (Spokane, WA). "Boise Jarred by Gun Fight." June 24 1907, 1.

Webb, Anna. "Features; Things That Go Bump in the Night." *Idaho Statesman*, October 28, 2003, 16.

6. The Haunted Prison Yard

Du Toit, J. (2015). "Idaho Prison Riot July 1980." YouTube. Idaho Department of Correction. Accessed February 20, 2023. https://www.youtube.com/watch?v=ezIbSR_ELVs.

Idaho Statesman. "Century-Old Idaho Penitentiary Faces Last Months." May 27, 1973, 39.

———. "Further Hearings, Research Asked on Location of New Penitentiary." March 16, 1963, 6.

Wade, J., and A. Sperry. ISCI Ghost Stories. Personal. November 10, 2022.

Wade, J., and Epps Griffin. ISCI Ghost Stories. Personal. October 8, 2022.

7. Those Haunted Hills

Idaho Statesman. "Died." December 27, 1875, 3.

———. "Footsteps of Idaho Ghosts." November 3, 1963, 4.

———. "Two Ghosts and a Shaggy Dog." *Idaho Statesman*, March 5, 1961, 4.

Morning Oregonian (Portland, OR), January 5, 1876, 1.

Western States Marriage Index. Brigham Young University–Idaho. Special Collections and Family History. http://abish.byui.edu/specialCollections/westernStates/search.cfm.

8. The Eighth Street Entity

Idaho Daily Statesman. "Elks Conduct Last Solemn Rites. Erastus W. Beemer." April 9, 1912, 2.

———. "Haunted House: An Uncanny Something in Mr. Black." November 15, 1892, 5.

———. "The Haunted House: Facts for the Superstitious." November 16, 1892, 5.

———. "Local." July 31, 1890, 4.

———. "Local Brevities." January 13, 1895, 6.

———. "Mortuary Notice." April 6, 1912, 2 A.

———. "Painful Accident." August 26, 1891, 8.

———. "Sad Termination." August 29, 1891, 8.

Idaho Statesman. "Idaho History: James H. Bush Invested in Horses." December 19, 2010.

9. Ghosts Travel: The Haunting of the Boise Little Theater

Camarda, Nicole. "Boise Little Theater's History Brings Spooky Spirits to Auditorium." *Idaho News 6.* October 29, 2020.

Idaho Architecture Project. "Boise Little Theater." Accessed February 17, 2023. https://www.idahoarchitectureproject.org.

Idaho Statesman. "Boise Little Theater Opens First Play in New Building." October 3, 1957, 6.

———. "Boise's New Little Theater Building Has Troubles, It Is Almost (But Not Quite) Ready to Open Doors." September 23, 1957, 6.

———. "Coroner Delays Decision on Little Theater Query." May 18, 1956, 14.

———. "Coroner Says No Inquest in Little Theater Tragedy." May 19, 1956, 3.

———. "Little Theater Is Completed during Year." January 1, 1958, 10.

———. "New Boise Little Theater Inspected by 1000 Guests." September 23, 1957, 6.

———. "Out of the Ashes in the Wake of Tragic Conflagration Another Boise Little Theater Project Must Rise Again." May 20, 1956, 4.

———. "Two Killed as Fire Razes Little Theater." May 1956, 1.

Ogden Standard-Examiner. "Funeral to Be Held Here for Ogdenite Killed in Fire." May 19, 1956

Randolph, June. State of Idaho Death Certificate, 1961.

10. Boise Embraces Satan

Idaho State Journal (Pocatello, ID). "Creech Case to Jury Soon." October 21, 1975, 7.

Idaho Statesman. "Boise Pastors Voice Beliefs about Devils." February 24, 1974, 18.

———. "Crusade Attracts 2,000 to Stadium in Caldwell." August 19, 1972, 20.

———. "Horse Mutilation Sets of Speculation about Occult." January 21, 1991.

Jones, Larry M. "Cult Crimes Impact Network, Inc." Idaho Secretary of State. October 14, 1994.

Times-News (Twin Falls, ID). "Mental Health Problems Saved Woman." July 12, 1994, 10.

Wade, J., and B. Bunger. Satanic Ritual at Jump Creek. Personal. July 30, 2022.

Woodward, Tim. "Mutilations Probe Focuses on Occult." *Idaho Statesman*, December 17, 1976, 64.

———. "Who, or What, Mutilates Cattle?" *Idaho Statesman*, July 6, 1975, 1.

Young, Darin. "A Satanic Cult Full of Witches…in Rathdrum, Idaho? Do Tell!" IdaHistory, October 4, 2022. www.idahistory.com.

11. What's That Noise in the Basement?!

Boise, Idaho City Directory. "Chas W. Bragunier." U.S. City Directories, 1822–1995. 1929.

———. "Pearl A. Bragunier." U.S. City Directories, 1822–1995. 1927.

Dark House Podcast. "Boise Murder House (ID) Feat. Actor Justin Long." September 7, 2022.

Charlotte (NC) Observer. "Fugitive from Mill Town." November 6, 1988, 1E.

Idaho Architecture Project. "Chop-Chop House." Accessed February 10, 2023. https://www.idahoarchitectureproject.org.

Idaho Daily Statesman. "Birdie E. Sexton Dies at Her Home." June 28, 1952.

———. "Guy Matthews." October 13, 1912, 4.

———. "John Eggan." Mar 14, 1958, 6.

———. "Spring Is 'Bustin Out All Over Pastoral Ivywild Community'." May 1, 1949, 36.

Idaho Statesman. "Accomplice in Dismemberment Case Freed." October 8, 1988, 19.

———. "Boisean Gets Five Years in Dismemberment Death." April 15, 1988, 20.

———. "Court Told Gun Bore Rogers' Prints." March 15, 1988, 20.

———. "Deal Frees Cox of Murder Charge." March 22, 1988, 5.

———. "Friend: Rogers Made Threat." March 12, 1988, 22.

———. "Mistrial Sought in Boise Murder Case." March 8, 1988, 17.

———. "Murder Suspect Cared for Foster Teens." July 8, 1987, 1.

———. "Police Discover Blood on Street in Southeast Boise." July 1, 1987, 32.

———. "Rogers' Bullet Identified in Skull." March 17, 1988, 25.

———. "Rogers Gets Life for Dismemberment Killing." August 27, 1988, 1.

———. "Rogers Gets 6 More Years." September 14, 1988, 25.

———. "Rogers Says Blood Sickens Him." March 18, 1988, 25.

———. "Screams Prompted Call to Police." September 4, 1987, 24.

———. "2 Boiseans to Stand Trial in Dismemberment." October 2, 1987, 24.

———. "Verdict: Rogers Guilty of Murder, Dismemberment." March 19, 1988, 1.

KBOI. "The Murder House: Is Site of Decades-Old Murder Haunted?" June 28, 2012. Accessed February 19, 2023. https://idahonews.com.

KEZJ. "Why You Can't Visit the Most Haunted House in Idaho." October 26, 2022. Accessed February 19, 2023. https://kezj.com.

Mercury News (San Jose, CA). "Murderer Got Custody of Boys." July 9, 1987, 6A.

State of Idaho Death Certificate. "Ellen Lyndsay Marker." July 20, 1959.

Supreme Court of Idaho, Daniel E. RODGERS, Petitioner-Appellant, v. STATE of Idaho, Respondent. Docket No. 22417. Decided January 23, 1997.

USA Today. "Despite a Prior Conviction For." July 7, 1987.

12. The Lost Souls of Fort Boise

Dillon, Wilma Collier. *Deaths and Burials Boise Barracks Military Reserve Idaho 1863–1913*. N.p.: self-published, 2003.

Hart, Arthur. "Old Boise Barracks Hospital Still Undergoes Remodeling." *Idaho Statesman*. May 17, 1976, 15.

Idaho Daily Statesman. "Barracks Hospital." January 22, 1909, 4.

———. "Boise Barracks Hums with Work of Preparation." March 21, 1920, 10.

———. "Boise Barracks: Their Origin, History and Possibilities for the Future." March 28, 1920, 1.

———. "Bury Them Deep." June 12, 1889, 3.

———. "Cadet Park in Cottonwood Gulch." January 24, 1902, 3.

———. "Captain William Yates Fatally Hurt by Horse." July 18, 1906, 5.

———. "Cemetery." September 1, 1976, 15.

———. "Died." November 30, 1886.

———. "Edward A. Cummings." September 14, 1897, 6.

———. "Epitaphs Tell Tragic Story of Maj. Collins' Family." June 1, 1976, 23.

———. "Fifty Years Ago." September 21, 1919, 6.

———. "Fire in the Hospital at the Barracks." January 19, 1900, 6.

———. "For Ex-Service Men." December 9, 1919, 6.

———. "Former Service Men at Barracks Celebrate Xmas." December 26, 1920, 3.

———. "From Ghostly Footsteps to Clint Eastwood, Mountain Cove High Has Seen It All." April 23, 2008, 2.

———. "Ft. Boise Battled More Whites than Redskins." September 21, 1969, 24.

———. "Graves Start Boisean on Quest." June 10, 1976, 38.

———. "Little-Known Garrison Field Holds Dramatic Tale of Gallant Major." September 9, 1945, 7.

———. "New Boise Barracks Hospital Modern, Up to Date, Institution." December 5, 1909, 7.

———. "Nurses Ready for Duty at Barracks Hospital." April 27, 1920, 5.

———. "Protection Wall for the Barracks—Cottonwood Flume." August 1, 1905, 3.

———. "Seeking Use of Barracks Hospital." January 25, 1915, 1.

———. "Soldiers Openly Protest Change." September 12, 1920, 3.

———. "Suicide." July 7, 1881.

———. "Suicide—Michael Healey." October 16, 1879, 3.

———. "Take a Halloween Tour of Haunted BOISE." October 25, 2005, 12.

———. "Trooper's Remains Are Laid to Rest." August 18, 1904, 5.

———. "Veterans Hospital Head Transferred." September 11, 1924, 4.

Idaho Sunday Statesman. "Footsteps of Idaho Ghosts." November, 1963, 4.

———. "Full Page." September 26, 1909, 5.

Idaho Tri-Weekly Statesman (Boise, ID). "Capt. Nickerson; Rev. W.R. Bishop." May 4, 1867, 2.

———. "Death Notices." September 16, 1869, 3.

———. "In Memoriam." September 18, 1869, 1

———. "Late Homicide." September 16, 1869, 2.

———. "Soldier Killed." September 14, 1869, 3.

Illingsworth, Gertrude Porter. "An Historical Study of the Establishment of Boise City and Fort Boise, Idaho." Master's thesis, n.d. On file at Idaho State Historical Society Library, Boise, Idaho.

Lugenbeel, Major Pinckney. "Letter to Daughter." Fort Boise, Idaho Territory, July 7, 1863.

Yoder, Miriam. *History of U.S. Veterans Hospital "52" Boise, Idaho*. March 25, 1947.

13. Project Grudge: Unidentified Flying Objects over the Boise Valley

Fold3. Project Blue Book—UFO Investigations. Accessed February 15, 2023. https://www.fold3.com.

Times-News. "Speedy 'Flying Saucers' Now Being Reported Throughout United States." June 7, 1947, 1.

About the Authors

Mark Iverson grew up in Seattle, Washington, where he followed bands like Soundgarden and Alice in Chains. Mark joined the Peace Corps and spent time in the Balkans. He moved to Idaho in 2009 and founded IdaHistory in 2019. He earned his master's degree in history from Boise State University. He is a huge rock music fan and collects vintage Star Wars toys that he tells his children not to touch.

Jeff Wade was born here in the greatest state of the Union. He holds a BS in criminal justice and has worked in public service for almost fifteen years. He published his first book, *Brave as a Lion: Jeff Standifer and the Knights of the Golden Circle*, in December 2019 and was the creator, cohost and producer of *Cascadia Podcast: History of the Pacific Northwest*. He loves modern metal music and listens to it constantly.

Learn about their local walking tours, research services, podcast and more at www.idahistory.com.

FREE eBOOK OFFER

Scan the QR code below, enter your e-mail address and get our original Haunted America compilation eBook delivered straight to your inbox for free.

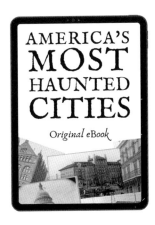

ABOUT THE BOOK

Every city, town, parish, community and school has their own paranormal history. Whether they are spirits caught in the Bardo, ancestors checking on their descendants, restless souls sending a message or simply spectral troublemakers, ghosts have been part of the human tradition from the beginning of time.

In this book, we feature a collection of stories from five of America's most haunted cities: Baltimore, Chicago, Galveston, New Orleans and Washington, D.C.

SCAN TO GET
AMERICA'S MOST HAUNTED CITIES

Having trouble scanning? Go to:
biz.arcadiapublishing.com/americas-most-haunted-cities

Visit us at
www.historypress.com